The Fullerton-SJI Leadership Lectures II

Lasallian Pathfinders

Of Ordinary Men and Less Ordinary Leadership

The Fullerton-SJI Leadership Lectures II

Lasallian Pathfinders

Of Ordinary Men and Less Ordinary Leadership

Editors

Arnold Gay
Vincent Anandraj

W⬧ World Scientific

NEW JERSEY • LONDON • SINGAPORE • BEIJING • SHANGHAI • HONG KONG • TAIPEI • CHENNAI

Published by

World Scientific Publishing Co. Pte. Ltd.
5 Toh Tuck Link, Singapore 596224
USA office: 27 Warren Street, Suite 401-402, Hackensack, NJ 07601
UK office: 57 Shelton Street, Covent Garden, London WC2H 9HE

Library of Congress Control Number: 2014951776

British Library Cataloguing-in-Publication Data
A catalogue record for this book is available from the British Library.

LASALLIAN PATHFINDERS
Of Ordinary Men and Less Ordinary Leadership

ISBN 978-981-4616-18-8

In-house Editor: Li Hongyan

Typeset by Stallion Press
Email: enquiries@stallionpress.com

Content

Lasallian Pathfinders
Of Ordinary Men and Less Ordinary Leadership

Foreword

Lessons from
The Fullerton-SJI Leadership Lectures II

⇨ **Arnold Gay**

It was midway through the lectures when a young man challenged me on leadership.

He noted that the guest speakers so far had included a scientist, a judge, and a musician, all with colourful life stories, but little to offer on leadership.

He had a point, after all, the traditional view of leadership is what I call the Lion — someone full of charisma, capable of raising armies and pushing people out of their comfort zones beyond the standards they set for themselves.

But that narrow definition would be a severe injustice to the seven men who shared their stories, and their lessons on life and leadership.

Politician, judge, scientist, educator, businessman, musician, and food guru.

You couldn't ask for a more diverse group of Josephians representing such a broad cross section of society today.

❖ Men Who Serve

Tellingly, in true Lasallian spirit, none saw themselves as either fitting, or worthy guest speakers. They agreed simply because they were called once again to share their experiences with a younger generation, and placed the community before themselves.

They are the kind of leaders who form the backbones of successful organisations. They seek neither personal glory nor the limelight, and give their all to make their teams better.

They are the leaders who will endure where others fade.

✤ Courage

It takes courage to be a man who serves, and Casino Regulatory Authority chairman Richard Magnus described this best, when he said leaders must be willing to get their hands dirty, sometimes even at the expense of their own private beliefs and convictions.

Courage is what KF Seetoh and Jeremy Monteiro had when they decided to forge their own paths in life.

Courage is what corporate chief Tony Chew had when he forayed into the great unknown, and Professor Leo Tan displayed that same spirit when he rebuilt the Singapore Science Centre.

⇨ Humility

For all their achievements, all who participated in the discussions are some of the most grounded men I have ever met. Philippine Education Secretary Brother Armin Luistro is a full Cabinet Minister, but he often travels alone and eschews hotels for more humble abodes offered by fellow brothers around the region.

Leadership author Jim Collins discovered that the difference between consistently high performing organisations and all others was the presence of humility in leadership.

He said such leaders were personally humble but fiercely ambitious for the good of their organisations and causes. Brother Armin wandered in the political wilderness for five years as he pursued justice for his people. Yet three years after he became the Education Secretary, his net worth was just $16,000. As Brother Armin puts it: "When you are poor, you are free, and I am the happiest Cabinet Minister."

⚜ Integrity

Leadership experts sometimes break this into two parts: honesty and credibility. The first value speaks for itself, but the second is worth touching on. I believe it goes beyond the conventional understanding of the word, and into a sense of solidness and consistency about the person. You know he is real, you can believe him and put your faith in him.

Tony Chew believes that a leader without integrity will never earn the trust of people around him, let alone lead them.

⟡ Care for Others

Say what you will about tough love, in the end, followers all want to know that their leaders and bosses actually care about them. It creates an environment where people can flourish.

A lack of care only attracts people either willing to be abused or enjoy learning how to become abusers.

✤ It's Not About Me

In a world of outsized egos, true leaders never make it about themselves. The men who took part in this series felt they were accountable; to their subordinates, followers, countrymen, professions, and God.

Call it a sense of stewardship, but ethical leaders don't just do whatever they want. They are always aware they are responsible to others.

The Lions and visionaries will have their place in society as leaders, but as Director of Development & Communications at SJI International, Vincent Anandraj, puts in his closing comments in this book: different and versatile people are behind the greatest football teams. And THAT is what the Lasallian community is all about.

It has been an honour to have moderated the sessions with the speakers of the Fullerton-SJI Leadership Lectures II.

Arnold Gay
Class of 1983

Professor

Leo Tan

∾

President and Fellow of the
Singapore National Academy of Science

A marine biologist by training, Professor Tan (Class of 1963) has for over 40 years made significant contributions to science education, youth development and conservation efforts in Singapore. In addition, Professor Tan is also the Chairman of the National Youth Achievement Award Council, Chairman of the Singapore Garden City Fund, Chairman of Singapore Technologies Endowment Programme, and Chairman of the Science Sub-Commission of the Singapore National Commission for UNESCO. He is also the Asia-Europe Foundation Governor for Singapore.

A recipient of numerous awards such as National Science & Technology Medal, The French National Order of Merit (Officer), Singapore National Day Award Public Administration Medal (Gold) (Bar), Singapore National Day Award Public Service Star and President's Award for the Environment, Professor Tan also served in various international organisations such as the Federation of Asian Scientific Academies & Societies, Pacific Science Association Committee on Science Communication & Education and the Science Council of Asia.

Professor Tan's interest in the education of school teachers and students began at the University of Singapore where he conducted marine ecology courses (on a voluntary basis) for teachers. This interest continued at the Singapore Science Centre (SSC) where he was Director and Chief Executive for 10 years. During his tenure at the SSC, he raised awareness and promoted understanding among students and the general public on the relevance of science and technology in their everyday lives, through non-formal science education and experiential learning. By the time he left, SSC was hailed as one of the top science museums in the world by the International Council of Museums.

From 1994 to 2006, Professor Tan was the Director of the National Institute of Education (NIE) at the Nanyang Technological University, responsible for the training of Singapore teachers from initial preparation to professional development. Some of his significant contributions at NIE include the establishment of a flagship research centre and the development of an internationally acclaimed leadership programme. Under his leadership, NIE grew to become an institute of distinction, highly regarded by its peers from the region as well as the UK, USA, Australia and the Middle East. Colleges of Education, based on the NIE model, were established in Abu Dhabi (2002) and Bahrain (2007) to which NIE was a turnkey consultant.

As the Director (Special Projects), Faculty of Science, National University

of Singapore (NUS), Professor Tan successfully championed the restoration of the 160 year-old Raffles Museum Natural History Collection. Under his leadership, a total of $56 million was raised for the building of the new Lee Kong Chian Natural History Museum at NUS. The museum, slated to open in 2015, will house three of the largest dinosaur skeletons (diplodocid sauropods), believed to be the most complete and articulated fossils discovered in the past century.

Professor Tan graduated from SJI in 1963 and currently serves as a member of the SJI Integrated Programme Track Leadership Panel.

Dr Koh Thiam Seng, Principal of SJI, Mr Vincent Anandraj, Chairman of the Fullerton-SJI Leadership Lecture Series, distinguished guests, ladies and gentlemen. It is very humbling to stand before the present SJI students, peers and alumni of SJI. I have been very privileged to have studied in one school from Primary One right through to Pre University (JC). Those days we went through Primary One, Primary Two, Standard One, Standard Two etc. I was always the slow student. Not six years of primary schooling but seven. That was the privilege we had, of building bonds because you knew everyone in the school for a very long time. And the teachers seldom changed, not because they had nowhere else to go but because they dedicated their lives to training the future, to educating the future at SJI. And that is my background.

I am here not so much to talk about leadership (which is the theme) but more about living a life. All my life I just wanted to be a marine biologist. That's because I saw in the movies Jacques Cousteau and the likes diving underwater swimming with the whales, sharks and so forth. It was fascinating. So I thought that was exactly what I

wished to do except I feared water and could not swim.

And so how does one become a marine biologist? If you are interested in something you chase your dream and I finally made it. And I spent 10 years of my life happily as a marine biologist. Up until one fateful New Year, I got a phone call from the Ministry of Education. In those days you got a call not because you did something right but probably because you did something wrong, you said something wrong. And it was very frightening because the caller said, "After the Chinese New Year you will come and see the minister," and that spoilt my new year completely because it was a four-day holiday over the weekend.

And over those four days, I wondered what I did wrong. And finally when I saw the minister, he said "I want you to leave the University and come to the Science Centre." In 1981 the Science Centre wasn't the Science Centre you see today. It was an outpost way out in rural Jurong. It took one and a half hours to get there from town. I later found out why the minister asked me to take over the reins of the Science Centre. My predecessor, the first local director was migrating to Australia and I wanted to find out why he was running away.

I only found out later that seven others before me (seven is a very nice number

in the Bible too) had cleverly found good reasons why they should not take over the running of the Science Centre. None of them were Josephians. And unfortunately, or fortunately, in all my years in SJI, I was always told to do as you are told. Rise to the challenge; accept whatever is given to you.

And so I became the reluctant 8th candidate who could not think of an excuse. At that time I thought the Science Centre was more of a liability than a gift. It was seen as a children's museum. Here I was, a young lecturer with a PhD, and I was being asked to run a children's museum. My professor from Japan flew down to Singapore and told me that there are only two types of people in Japan who take up museum directorships. One is when you are about to retire — I was 38 years old.

Two, your boss did not think very much of you. It was very demoralising. Nevertheless I thought about it for one whole month. And the minister called me again and asked, "Well, have you made up your mind?" And I said "Yes! Can I go there on trial for two years and if I don't like it, go back to the university?" And he said, "No! It takes two years to teach you the ropes, for you to learn the ropes. Another two years for you to give back, so that's at least four years. I said, "Ok, if that's the case, four years." Remember that SJI instilled in me the belief that duty comes first.

Those four years became ten years. I found that the minister had handed me a gem, a gold nugget wrapped up in brown paper and I didn't recognise it. Remember, I was a marine biologist, who could not swim? I had no idea how to run an organisation and I was suddenly thrown into the deep end to lead 100 people who first looked at me and said, "Huh? This guy knows nothing about museums." And I was at the mercy of 100 people who knew what they were doing but I didn't and I was supposed to lead them. How do you do that?

The first thing I did was to ask them, "What is the purpose of this organisation?" They told me, and I said, "Very good". And I asked "How do you intend to use exhibits to display science and technology in a way that will excite the young?" They explained to me all the various things that we had to do. And they also told me that I had to raise plenty of money as the government did not give a single cent for exhibit development in those days. I said "Ok, sounds like I have to run away very soon. But what is it that attracts people to your exhibits? What is it that would capture their imagination?" They showed me a few exhibits and I said, "Very good, provided that

people come to see these exhibits, they will get excited. If they don't, how do you know that they will stay to see/look at your other exhibits?" Then I asked, "What is the one thing that every visitor who comes to the Science Centre would want to visit or has to visit?" They looked puzzled. And I said, "Don't you go to the loo every day?" And they said, "What do you mean?" I said, "Science."

You tell me that you want to show how relevant science is in our everyday lives. And the first place I want to visit if I have to travel one and a half hours is the loo. What if I can pique the curiosity of the visitor while he is in the washroom? I knew that very few people know how the flush system works. What if you were to cut a hole in the plastic cistern, fix a transparent window across the cut to show how as they pull the chain, the ball falls as the water flows down and then, and as the water refills again, it pushes up the ball to block the inlet pipe and have an explanation about how science works in your house, in your toilet. And that was the beginning of a very fascinating journey I found of getting people to listen to what I had to say even though I didn't know then what exhibitions were all about, I learnt how to develop an exhibition by using the innate curiosity which was inculcated in school, about finding answers that do not lie in textbooks, but learning that the seeds of the solution could be found by thinking about the problem itself.

And that was when I began to get a little respect from my staff and they said. "This guy is not that bad after all. He is not so ignorant after all. Maybe we can follow him." And ten years later, when I left the Science Centre it was one of the top ten Science Centres in the world. It wasn't because I knew my job; it is because my people knew their job. They knew what they were doing and I knew I had to provide the resources including the money. I had to support them; whenever they suggested an idea I didn't pour cold water on it. I'd say, "Put it in our Ideas Bank. Every Monday we will examine which ones could be adopted and which to be shelved. It is important to justify why you think your idea will work and if the management team agrees, we will develop it into an exhibition." And that was a little journey of an institution where our staff had no promotional prospects elsewhere in the civil service. It was a single career at the Science Centre. You started and ended your career there and the salary was below market rate but it was a place full of fun and experiential learning. You could devise your own toys. You could devise your own exhibits and use your imagination to excite other people about science and technology. And that was the inspiration.

So what did that teach me? It taught me to always put people first; in anything that you do you do not ask, what is the objective, how do I get more visitors in? You start by looking at your own people in your organisation and say, "You are the most important people. You know what you are doing and I will trust you. I will listen to you and will give you necessary support and I will be your 'ra-ra' cheerleader." I do not know how to build an exhibition but I do know what needs to be supported. And secondly think about your profession. How to be professional, honest, have integrity and do the best you can. You should also scan the horizon and scour for the latest or futuristic discoveries, innovations and applications in S & T for exhibition themes, to convey the wonderment of what you are trying to show. And thirdly, that is where you measure their performance. I do not mean the establishment

THE FULLERTON HOTEL
SINGAPORE

of KPIs such as "There must be 6 exhibitions a year, there must be so many visitors per month," which they can deliver very easily. We can look at these KPIs anytime. But are they meaningful performance indicators? It is only when your staff have a sense of ownership in their work and believe in what they are doing, that you have a followership. Only then can you become a leader. And so I learnt how to understand what my staff needs were and the Science Centre became a popular place. When I left, there were about a million visitors per year.

But why did I leave the Science Centre? I was beginning to enjoy myself there because I managed to master the ropes, so to speak. Having said that, my bosses had another job for me at the newly established National Institute of Education of Nanyang Technological University. A friend said, "Leo, you are enjoying yourself too much. Work mustn't be so enjoyable so they are sending you somewhere else." And this was a place that I didn't want to go to. If you recall, I told you — I dreaded water and I couldn't swim but became a marine biologist. I didn't think much of museums because they were for retirees to run and I was given that task. So I told myself, if I could change the attitude of the public towards the Science Centre, maybe this new offer of how to educate teachers might not be too bad after all, but a previous IE Director told me, "Leo, if you take on this job, you will be blamed not only by the teachers and the students but by the parents and by everybody in society because in their eyes, the Institute of Education always trained the wrong kinds of teachers." And true enough, several of my friends didn't want to talk to me when they heard I was going to NIE because they were too shy to tell me that their children wanted to become teachers. They avoided me. That was the state of affairs in 1990.

But NIE was going to be a part of the new university, NTU, so when another minister asked me to go, I said, "Well, I had a grubby piece of paper before which hid a gem within and maybe this will also be a gem." Since I had been an armchair critic of what was lacking in our education system, the only way to address it was to jump right into the hot seat. And I accepted, but there was allure this time. Everyone knew I valued an academic career and I was given the vague promise that I could become Dean of Science in ten years when NTU would start its College of Science. All I had to do was to work ten years in NIE and I would be placed back in the university mainstream. I wanted to get back to marine biology, so it was music to my ears to hear I could return.

But that promise of a change of direction never materialised. I stayed for 18 years in NIE and it was more challenging in NIE because everyone there has a PhD or Master's degree. And when you're the director you are not the boss. You are the facilitator. They will tell you "Yes, we will follow you", but like cats they would go off in whichever direction they wished. And I realised if I were to follow the

old traditional way of running the NIE there will be no future for the teachers because these professors would all want to do their research and forget about the teaching part. And therefore we have to find a way to thin out the hierarchical chain and have a flat matrix system. But that wasn't easy. When we did a survey, the majority of the staff was very sceptical or cynical about whether a flat structure would work for an institution which did not have departments to belong to and so forth. And so what do you do? I never went to management school. The only thing I knew was that I should listen to dissenters. You identify them, the naysayers, the ones who say the opposite of what you think, is the way to go. And this is another management or leadership skill that I learned along the way, that you put people first. The naysayers, the devil's advocates, are what you need to stay awake, because it is in adversity that your real leadership skills and talents come through. In an organisation where everybody agrees with you, how would you know when you are going down a slippery slope?

And in NIE I was looking for those who were the most vocal and said that they didn't think that the matrix system of organisation, that of a flat structure, would work. And of course you would first pick a chairman who believes in the objective. You cannot

pick a chairman who says no first. But your committee members must be made up of some people whose beliefs are 180-degrees from yours. I was introduced to this idea in national service. I found that obedient rank and file servicemen had greater difficulty getting promoted. However, the more brash and defiant ones seemed to be more favoured for promotion to lieutenant and inspector. I thought there must be a logic to this. When these somewhat wayward servicemen assumed positions of responsibility, they found that they could not behave the way they did previously. They now had people under their charge and therefore they changed their behaviour and that is why I included two of my five taskforce members who didn't think the system would work. I told them, "Choose any place in the world with such a system and I will send you there. When you come back, tell us in a report why the system cannot work." But of course I knew that when they came back, the chances were that they would change their minds, having seen it work in the educational institutes they visited. And that, they did. We also conducted surveys among the staff to gauge their willingness for change. At first 30% said yes. In the second survey several months later, it went up to 50% and by the third, it was 75% who said, "Yes, we think we can change to the new system."

Why am I talking about these adversities? I found that in today's world we are always looking for the path of least resistance, the easiest or most expeditious way to get things done and we forget about the true purpose of education. The fundamentals are about character building, honesty; holistic education develops the mind, the body, the heart and the soul. And this is something that is fundamental, and which has never changed. Our founder, John Baptist De La Salle, never intended to found an Order, he just wanted to teach, wanted to start a normal school to train teachers, but he didn't know he was destined to start the Lasallian order which had a mission to go all throughout the world to educate, first, the poor, and now it is not just those who cannot afford it, but everybody.

I found that when you are thrown into the deep end, your survival instinct kicks in. Somehow you will never sink. But if you are not thrown into the deep end, you will never go beyond yourself and take calculated risks in decision-making and instead choose the softer options. Why risk failure and incur reduced promotional prospects? But is that being honest to yourself? Is that integrity? Is that about shaping the world around you? You see, greatness is not about trying to change the world but rather just doing your job the best you can, understanding what your role is within the spheres that you are able to influence and let others worry about the rest. The advancement of our society depends on little actions we do in our daily lives, such as Learning by Doing and Sharing by Example.

When I get volunteered for lots of things, my first reaction is to say no. But on the other hand when you say yes, you get to learn new things, new skills. Skills which you think are not useful for your current job but actually the things you do outside of your job is what teaches you how to do your current job better. This is a paradox. And the busier you are, the more things you can get done, rather than saying, "I have enough tasks, please don't disturb me anymore." So don't simply refuse when somebody comes to you with an offer which doesn't seem attractive, at all meaningful or relevant to you, but which will become relevant as you move along the chain. Didn't Confucius say, "Choose a job you love, and you will never work a day in your life."? That's how I started being a marine biologist because enjoying nature was my hobby and therefore, when I became a marine biologist, it wasn't a job; it was somebody paying me to enjoy my hobby.

When I went to the Science Centre and to NIE, those were not tasks I wanted;

they were things that were thrust upon me and I tried to resist. However, once I accepted the opportunity, there was no turning back and I could not say, "Now I don't want to do a proper job". You're going to do it to the best of your ability and turn your job into a hobby and that's what I did. I turned my Science Centre and NIE jobs into hobbies and then it wasn't work either. And when I finally stepped out of NIE, that was when I said, "Now I want to get back to marine biology, my first love." But alas, it was not to be because when I went back to NUS, the first thing I asked myself was: why is there still an unfinished task at NUS?

Forty years ago, when I was a young lecturer, I was present when specimens from the National Museum, which was across the road from SJI, were being discarded. We managed to salvage a few hundred thousand specimens which have been kept as a research and teaching resource at NUS for the last 40 years. But that was the legacy, the national heritage of Singaporeans. It belonged to the people of Singapore. Why is it that they did not have the right to go back and visit the National History Museum? So I asked NUS president, Prof Tan Chorh Chuan, for permission to resurrect the museum and he told me, he said, "Leo, our duty is to teach and do research, not to run a public museum. If you want a public museum, you will have to raise thirty-five million dollars, but I will give you a site on campus to build the museum." In a daze, I said "Done!"

He added, "And by the way, you have six months to do it".

Six months? But I had given my word. Like good SJI boys, we always keep our word, do or die, we finish the job. And in six months' time, five of us delivered $46 million to Prof Tan Chorh Chuan and we said, "Please give us the land to build a new museum which you will see in 2014."

So the essence of leadership is not about leading people. It's about getting out there and doing what you can, what you think cannot be done. But

nothing is impossible until it is proven to be impossible and failure is not an option. That was what my Irish Brothers taught me. They caned me; corporal punishment was the order of the day, and I never complained to my parents, reported it to the police or whoever else, because I got a second caning if I told them a Brother had caned me that morning. So I remember that discipline, honest hard work and using creativity — which the Lasallian spirit embodies — is embedded in the culture of La Salle. Using the creativity which is ingrained in us, to the fullest of our ability would ensure that first, we will have a bright future, second, our society will have a bright future, and third, our country and the world will be a better place to be in. Thank you very much.

Forum

Arnold Gay: When you were talking about your past experiences, you brought up Prof Tan Chorh Chuan. He spoke at this series as well and he made a very interesting point about "useless knowledge". When I was in school, there were days when all I did was ask, "Why am I listening to this stupid lecture? Why am I not out there, you know, playing football? Why am I not doing something that's more relevant to me?" What do you say to the many boys and girls who will surely will asking those same questions at some point in their lives?

Leo Tan: The key is always to have fun. This is one thing that Christian Brothers' Schools never permitted in my time. When I went to school, it was a very serious place. The playground was our refuge of freedom and that's why we played during recess and after hours. That was the time we had our real fun. But in school, in class, if so much as a smirk appeared on your face, you could be punished because learning was a serious thing and internally I was a rebellious kid, though externally I was very obedient. And as a result, my teachers never knew what I was thinking about them when they were being strict disciplinarians but I thought if ever I get a chance when I grow up, if I'm ever in a position of power, I am going to make sure that my colleagues and I have fun working, no matter how difficult the situation is. Only when you are having fun then the right endorphins flow in your body and when you are happy, you can think of solutions. When you are unhappy and worried, how do you study for your exams? How do you solve the work problems that your boss has given you? Because you're worried about worry itself! And this is the trick in telling yourself, "I'm going to have fun." Fun doesn't mean being irresponsible, not doing the task at hand but rather, this is my way of addressing the issue.

think is right (sorry teachers, principal) you have to be very, very clear why you are doing what you are doing and you must be prepared to answer fully for the consequences of your action, and not shift the blame and not, "He told me to do it, it's his fault." It is my responsibility. If I say I am going to do it, I will accept responsibility for the failure and not my subordinate or my friends, unless you all collectively signed a blood pledge stating that you will take the blame for something.

So on "useless knowledge", actually Chorh Chuan was right. I will give you the story of Professor Frederick Dainton, who was invited to do a controversial thing in Singapore. He helped merge Nanyang University and Singapore University to form the National University of Singapore in 1981, and again in 1991, he was instrumental in merging the College of Physical Education, the Institute of Education and Nanyang Technological Institute to create Nanyang Technological University. So twice he played a very important role. Prof Dainton was a chemist. He was chosen by then PM Lee Kuan Yew to help facilitate the merger of two universities and the formation of a new university. But as a chemistry lecturer, he was not popular with his students because he taught them all kinds of "useless" Chemistry, or at least that's

Give me a chance to try my way of solving the problem. You will be surprised at how productive and efficient our organisation can be. I have proved in two organisations that it is possible. That's because I was given the responsibility to be the CEO. If I were not the CEO, it would have been impossible. Without the support of the top, your juniors cannot execute what they want to do because you will always say, "Stop, how do you know it will work?" I was always told to ask for permission, but I found asking for forgiveness was much easier. If you want to do something you

student had graduated, he came back to him and said, "Professor Dainton, you have just saved my life today, 15 years after I graduated from Sheffield." And he asked, "What did I do?" The student said, "I was always criticising you for giving us irrelevant information but today at the refinery, my boss asked me to identify the plausible cause of the problem. And I immediately thought of what you asked of me 15 years ago, which was useless to me then but today became the thing that saved my life and I think I'm going to get a promotion too because my boss thinks I'm so smart."

So you see, whatever bits of information you pick up along the way is never wasted. I'm a marine biologist. Whatever I learnt in marine biology has principles which I can use in dealing with people. Now I communicate with animals which cannot talk, which cannot explain to me what they do, so I have to fathom why they behave in certain ways and I used the same methods to observe people. I tell you, on the bus, in the train or at work, and they don't realise this but I'm sizing them up as they are sizing me up and I find that my marine biology training useful in observing people and society, drawing some inferences, maybe not the right conclusions, but these are very helpful in any work you do. I always tell trainee teachers at NIE that the most

what the students thought when he was teaching in Sheffield. He later became the Vice Chancellor, was knighted and promoted to the House of Lords. He told me, "I usually do this to my students, when I call them up to see me. I put some unfamiliar crystal or substance on the table and then I ask them to describe to me what it is and of course it stumps them completely." And so they leave his room grumbling, "This silly professor. He always asks me stupid questions which are neither in the syllabus nor the exam. What good is it?" He continued, saying that 15 years after a particular

important discipline they really need to master is psychology. Understanding who you are dealing with, whether it is your boss, your peer or your student, allows for you to communicate with each other. Communication is the first step towards understanding and resolving issues.

Arnold: On the subject of being all inclusive, in my line of work, when a new boss comes in, the number one thing he will do is he will boot out all the people who don't agree with him, and brings with him his entire team. You have a very different approach. You bring in the

people who don't agree with you. From the top all the way down to the bottom, equal time, equal space, equal attention. Please explain this concept here to everyone here and to me as well.

Leo: Very simple. All my initial bosses were always autocratic, disciplinarian or are more "old school". My head of department never saw me other than as a student. He taught me for four years at university, I left him for my PhD but when I came back, he was still there and he treated me as if I was a freshman, and that I should always be at his beck and call. Whichever lecture he didn't like, he passed to me. And he didn't know that he was doing me a favour because I didn't know what genetics was all about but since I had to teach, I was only seven hours ahead of the students and therefore I went to a class with just seven hours' knowledge of what I was going to lecture outside of my marine biology field. But those were the kinds of situations that force you to realise that actually you can learn new things. Old dogs can learn new tricks and I again realised that nasty bosses are very good for me. They taught me what I shouldn't be to other people but at the same time, because I had these bad experiences with my bosses, I learnt that I should be nice to people.

And the first thing I do when I go to an organisation is to get to know the people. You do not remove anybody. Yes, a senior alumnus once told me, "First thing I do when I go in is to bring all my people with me, the rest all get out." But I said, "That's your style. My style is all inclusive because everyone has a use, has a talent." Now, how do they make use of those talents? Yes, there are many parts of that person we might not like but there are parts that are useful to your organisation and this isn't to say that at the Science Centre I shouldn't sack any of the hundred employees, they were all civil servants and they have nowhere else to go to, so either I became guilty

of removing somebody's rice bowl or I try to make him more productive than he was. And once you take that positive attitude and the staff know that, they respond.

Even the wild animals will respond to your signals. I have bumped into snakes twice in my life. The first time I ran into a snake was when I was young. I lived in a ramshackle house with a garden, and I ran straight into a cobra and it reared up, ready to strike. I froze, I couldn't go forward, I couldn't go backwards and I had no time to be frightened. What do you do? You look at the creature even though it could spit its venom straight at you and blind you. I looked at it and it looked at me. We stayed stationary for a while, and I began summoning a voice that whispered "Slowly, slowly, walk backwards." That was the longest walk backwards I ever had in my life but I got out of the snake's way and it didn't attack. The second time — and the textbooks, every textbook I read says snakes are dangerous — the second time I was swimming at Raffles Lighthouse. I encountered a sea snake. A sea snake is even more poisonous than a cobra because if it bites you, you have got to get an anti-venom injection within one hour of the bite or you're dead. And out at sea it takes at least two, three hours to get back to the mainland. And you drown before you even realise what has they had gone through several iterations and processes where everybody agreed that they were a detriment to the organisation or to themselves, only then did we remove them. But usually we will try to make the best use of the capabilities that God gave them. Why do we condemn people? Because we think that they are useless? When you tell a student he's stupid, he behaves stupidly but if you tell him, "Hey, I think you are smarter than what you have delivered in the exam," the chances are that he will prove to himself and then to you that he is, after all, bright.

Audience: In today's climate when we speak of leaders and we speak of success stories, a lot of people have very contradictory views of ambition and where it can bring a man. What are your views on ambition and would you say that you are an ambitious person?

Leo: Ambition is a good thing. Everyone must have an ambition. It is to what degree that you want to fulfil that ambition. Hitler was very ambitious. La Salle was very ambitious. It depends on whether the society feels that kind of ambition is something that they should aspire to. But if you are not ambitious you'll be like a couch potato, very happy to sit back and do nothing and watch the world go by, be a dreamer. However, there is a caveat. Not all dreamers stop

happened. We were swimming towards each other. We both turned away from each other simultaneously. I couldn't outswim it, but it proved to me that that snake thought that I was dangerous too. And that was when I began to understand communication with animals, they are just as frightened as we are and they don't attack you unnecessarily.

And it is the same with people. When you think of them as responsive to change, they will hopefully rise to the challenge. So for the 100 people, I never removed a single staff member unless there, it is important to be a dreamer because the best ideas come when you are dreaming. Walt Disney was a dreamer. He believed if you can dream it, you can do it. He started his career as an impoverished artist until this little mouse came along and he just doodled that mouse. It became Mickey Mouse. So, that dream became the reality. His ambition, I don't think, was to become a rich man but he did. And so the key is, what contentment is, one of the key factors that actually goes with ambition. If you have been blessed with the talent to be the Prime Minister of the country and when given the opportunity you refuse, then you are not living up to the ability that has been given to you. But if you are very content, think that being a private citizen is the right thing to be, nobody can fault you for it.

Audience: Hi, I graduated from SJI last year, I'm at ACJC right now. Nowadays we often hear a lot of stories in the papers and from teachers as well, students maybe, about how our education system is so stressful and forces students to conform. But at the same time, I mean, the rigour we have and the opportunities we have been given give us a little bit of an edge in the international world we live in now. As someone who has worked in NIE and maybe even

as someone, as you described yourself, who was once "a rebellious kid", I was wondering whether you could share with us what your views are, where the balance between having fun and being creative in education and having a lot of rigour lies in today's society.

Leo: Stress is a thing of modern society but you know, I think our ancestors had greater stress. Those who migrated from China, India and the archipelago, they had nothing but the shirts on their back, they were just thinking about survival. That's the greatest stress you can have in your life. How many of us are at the survival level, at that basic level of need? We have passed that stage and yet we feel so stressed. But you know in animals, the ones that are stressed actually lead longer lives. They are thinner, you stress them with no food but they have got longer lives. The fat ones, obese ones, are the ones that die very early and are full of disease. So there's a lot of corollary here and we've something to learn from the animal kingdom. Mr Lee Kuan Yew, our first prime minister, never allowed us a moment, those of our generation, never allowed us a moment to think that all was well in the world because he knew that we were frogs in a well. Singapore is the tiny red dot. He knew that the moment we had arrived, we are at that first world stage, people would start to take things for granted, just like we how we assumed the MRT would never break down, right? Business goes on. But you know a 25-year-old system must break down unless you maintain it well. But not so much like if you go to England now, they break down every day, there're several trains breaking down, but nobody writes to the press. In Singapore, half an hour and the whole world knows about Singaporeans complaining. So he understood that complacency breeds degeneration, decline, but stress must be healthy

stress, not unhealthy stress, and sometimes it's self-inflicted. Examinations, if you do your work on a regular basis [are less stressful], of course, as I'm the "11th hour" type too, but I believe that so you're only stressed right before the exam.

Now, in my time, regardless of whether you were Taoist, Hindu or Catholic or Christian we all went to the chapel to pray in exam time to relieve the stress. Stress is essential for our skeletal muscles. If the muscles are not stretched or extended, they don't contract well. Same thing with the psyche of the human mind. It's only when you think you have some stress that you put your real power to maximum or optimum usage. And that is why we have adrenaline in our system, but you do not want it flowing 24 hours a day because that would also lower your resistance to disease. And so where is the balance? I know that it's hard for you, you have only one worry — how to finish the syllabus, how to pass the exam. So when students tell me they are stressed, I say to them, "Wait till you go out and work, income tax, mortgage payments on a condo, car, credit card, then you've got children, how to send them to the right school, when they get sick, how do you take care of them." Then you will realise the full meaning of stress but as what one of my teachers, Brother Vincent (he was

my Primary 4 form teacher) taught me, "Each year it gets only this much more difficult, expect it, don't expect it to get easier but your brain is growing bigger. God gave you the ability to cope with the extras that will come." And in life, never give up because if you persist, you will succeed but if you are half-hearted, you will fail. And the key lies in your responsibility to eat healthily, exercise and study regularly.

So, at this level, when students tell me they are stressed I always scratch my head and say, "You know what, they are talking about different kinds of stress." But yes, those who come from fractured families have personal problems, those are a different kind and that needs special counselling and that's out of the ordinary. But the normal activities you mentioned, in response to my question that most of the time Christians and Taoists all go together to the chapel and pray to do well in the examinations. That sounds like a very healthy practice. But nowadays, if you are in a mission school for two years or six, I see that

increasingly we don't want religion to be part of education when parents say that schools should not teach the children about religion and at the same time, the Chairman of the Board believes that there has to be some element of religion in schools. As someone who has been involved in education, I often wonder, where should the balance lie?

Arnold: And this is a good question, Prof Tan. Old SJI had a role in making you the person you are today, what roles do you see for SJI and the De La Salle Brothers' schools in society today?

Leo: Since its inception, the government made it very clear it wanted to draw the line between secularism and religiosity because in Singapore, we are multi-religious, multi-cultural and keeping the harmony is an ongoing journey. It doesn't mean we have succeeded. By finely dividing what we could and could not do, the government initially banned all catechism. They then relented and said that mission schools could teach catechism after school hours and so on and so forth. Dr Goh Keng Swee introduced moral education, understanding the different faiths and so on. Each of us can find a balance in approach, each school, each mission school would have to define what it considers the right way because you admit students of other races, of other religions as well which is a very good thing. And that was the

strength of the old schools, of RI, ACS and SJI in those days. While we came from diverse backgrounds, we saw each other not as brown, black, yellow, we saw each other as school children, friends having fun with each other. We went home, we went to our separate temples, churches, whatever it was, but in school, the chapel was a place of quiet repose. We never saw it as an exclusive Christian God in there but adults have made it such that they teach their children from very young that there is this distinction and so forth.

Children are always very innocent. We grew up accepting each other for what

we were, and not for what our parents believed in. But today you can't turn back the clock, it has happened, and therefore as a mission school, you find within your curriculum time, a chance to say your prayers and hear about God. Those who do believe may be excused. Yet I have had non-Catholic parents telling me they appreciated their children imbibing values from our schools. One Muslim parent actually told me at CJC, "I don't mind my daughter attending your assembly where you say a prayer, she doesn't have to recite your prayer or believe in your god but that is the culture of the school that I send her to because I want her to imbibe some of these values as an individual," and that's the strength actually of our mission schools. It is not to proselytise, to recruit. Some Christian groups do that but Catholics are actually the most apathetic ones. You look at it and we are always accused of being non-Christians by many of our Christian friends because they say, "You never go out, catch people and make them believe in your faith." Gone are the days of the past, you can't do that anymore. We now lead by example.

This is what the spirit of the Lasallian character is. What makes you, a Josephian, different from any other school right away? What makes you stand out, special? It is not words; it is not explicit documents that say we are this, we are that. People just watch what you do in everyday life; it is as simple as that. Do you walk the talk? They watch you, they observe you and they decide whether you have the Ora et Labora spirit in you. You will recall in our school song, "sons of St Joseph valiant and true", this is a motto that I was brought up on and till today, even some of my friends who never converted to Catholicism, remember that this was the school that we imbibed values and really enjoyed ourselves in. And that reminds me of what one of my Sindhi friends said, "Eh, remember or not? Exam time we pray like mad. Like buy insurance if we didn't study hard enough."

Audience: In our lives, whether in school or work, there are some people who, despite their hard work and their knowledge, cannot succeed. What advice could you give to these people who may see themselves or their work as being futile?

Leo: This comes back to ambition. Sometimes there is misplaced

and you get disillusioned, the key is to note what is the appropriate route for you. There is vocational training. Today the ITEs produce magnificent students who are not academically bright but they achieve far more than some of their academically brighter peers.

In other words, it is about finding the right niche, right peg for the right hole and vice versa. As for those thoughts which go through the minds of many people who are disillusioned, is it self-pity? Is it really because the whole world is against them? Because today you go to the shelters, you'll find that a lot of these handicapped people, their skills are put to great use, making things with their hands, or even with their mouths they can operate a computer and be telephone operators or whatever. So they feel a sense of worth. The key is not all of us were born lucky, to get ahead in life in a normal sense. But whatever talent we have, we try to make use of it. I can understand there are a lot of misplaced people but when we go to the Ministry of Manpower and we look at the number of jobs and the number of people who are waiting for jobs, we find that a lot of those people who actually can do those jobs don't want to do those jobs because they think they don't pay well. The key is to start wherever you are, if you cannot get what you want, start where you are. People will spot you if you've got talent,

ambition — people telling you that you should be this, you should be that, and you find yourself a square peg in a round hole. We have seen at the National Youth Achievement Award (NYAA), that people with no limbs, they can kayak around the whole island, they can climb mountains and yet able-bodied people find it very difficult to do so. It is all about finding the right niche, finding the right mould. If you are not academically inclined and want to pursue a diploma in electrical engineering or what, and you are not good at it, if you are medio-cre, there are a hundred others better, if you are good at it and then you'll move up the chain. But if you don't start, then nobody will ever spot your talent and that I think is the greatest waste.

Singapore, actually our unemployment rate should be much lower than what it is because there are jobs going around but we are very particular in the types of jobs we choose. I'm not talking about handicapped people, I'm just talking about ordinary graduates from university who think, "Must be $3000, then I take it; anything less I don't want." But then you look at Hong Kong, you look at all the countries around us, their graduates who succeed are always those who never got guaranteed opportunities in the civil service or establishments where they start their first job. The people who came back to help me when I was in Singapore University were the students who failed their first year. In my time, as a lecturer I had the odious duty courtesy of my head of department, to inform students who failed their first year of their expulsion from the University. He gave me this duty as I was the most junior staff. But this is why I say he did me a favour because I learnt the psychology of how to deal with students who were sobbing and crying and bringing their parents and asking me to give them a second chance, a third chance and the university only permitted them one supplementary exam. After your April exam, the June exam, if you fail, you're out.

And three years later, the students are driving Mercedes Benzes back to the university and watching their honours classmates doing their honours level and they come and say, "Eh, I'm a *towkay* (a boss) already you know, why are you guys still studying so hard?" Why? Because in adversity they had no choice but to start as a contractor, do whatever they could and they made it good without a degree. So another key to life is — nobody owes us a living. That's another lesson I learnt from my botany professor. He never taught me any botany. That is I never remembered what he taught me as a physiologist but I remembered him for one thing. He said, "Leo, nobody owes you a living. If you get it, good for you. If you don't get it, go and find something else but you are responsible to yourself." And that is another lesson that I learnt.

Audience: I was just wondering since there's so much amazing thought on parenting, the importance of parents in society and the importance of education, why don't schools teach parenting in what they do?

Leo: The teachers would resign immediately. Okay you raised a pertinent point but even then there are certain things that are not the responsibility of the school. Parenting is a social, community responsibility. It belongs outside of the school because in school, teachers are more concerned with developing young minds, especially in the formative years from Primary One to Primary Six, where the last thought on the teachers' minds is about parenting. But don't be surprised if your young child teaches you something about about parenting. I believed in being a strict disciplinarian to my primary school-going children and my second boy told me, "I'm going to be a lawyer when I grow up. Watch out!" So I say, he knows his rights. Secondly, he said, "When I become a parent, I hope I will be more gentle with my children." So don't underestimate yourselves, and observe what people do, compare, but at that stage, it is not your responsibility to think of parenthood. Your responsibility is to pass examinations and please your parents. That's the first thing so that they know they've invested well in you. But the key is, I don't think it's fair to ask a school teacher to have a special class to teach the graduating class how to change diapers, how to be good parents and which school to send their children to, and so forth. There are more important things for you at that age.

Richard Magnus

Chairman
Casino Regulatory Authority

Richard Magnus is an SJI Alumnus (1963). He is a recently retired Senior District Judge (now termed the Chief District Judge).

In recognition of his sterling contributions to the nation, he was conferred the Public Administration Medal (Silver) in 1983, the Public Administration Medal (Gold) in 1994, the Public Administration Medal (Gold) (Bar) in 2003 and the Meritorious Service Medal in 2009.

He holds several public positions: Singapore's First Representative to the ASEAN Intergovernmental Commission on Human Rights; Chairman, Casino Regulatory Authority; Chairman, Public Guardian Board; Chairman, Political Films Consultative Committee; Chairman, Bioethics Advisory Committee (BAC); and Member of the Public Service Commission; Member, Public Transport Council; and Expert Member of UNESCO's International Bioethics Committee.

In the private sector, Richard sits on the Board of Directors of Temasek Cares PLC, CapitalMall Trust and the Changi Airport Group.

He has also edited five law books for legal practitioners. He is an Honorary Fellow of the Centre for the Study of Christianity, Trinity Theological College.

Richard initiated a community social and support programme for the citizens in South East Singapore which has been making good progress for some 12 years now. Richard is still busy being very active with social and welfare programmes in Cambodia and Indonesia; something he has been passionate about for several years.

SJI laid the foundation for his worship of God which reinforces and enriches his love of Singapore and respect for Singapore's founding fathers and leaders.

Richard, who graduated with an LLB (Honours) and LLM from the National University of Singapore, is also an alumnus of the Harvard Business School (Advanced Management Program) and the John F. Kennedy School of Government (State and Local Government Program).

Effective and Ethical Leadership: My Experiences

I thought I would share with you today, in broad terms, the relationship between effective and ethical leadership. Can ethics and being effective be mutually reinforcing rather than be in conflict? Many eminent persons in this lecture series have spoken on effective leadership; so I will be more inclined on the ethics component. The central issue is not one of style. John Kotter (who taught me Leadership and Change at the Harvard Business School's Program), in his book *What Leaders Really Do*, said that he conducted 14 formal studies and more than a thousand interviews. He often hears people say that we need a new leadership style for this century. In a globalising world with a better educated workforce and constituency that is no longer inclined to be seen and not heard, a new leadership is in fact called for, but style is not the key leadership issue. Substance is. It is about core behaviour on the job, not surface detail and tactics, a core that changes little over time, across different cultures, or in different industries or societies. Ethics, to me, is an essential core.

Being effective is about being able to influence others; to have an impact.

A large prerequisite of this is that you must have the power to do so.

Remember now what Lord Acton said: power corrupts.

Being ethical is to recognise virtues which are worthy of honour and recognition by the community, such as integrity, citizenship, service and moral limits. Aristotle identified courage, justice, prudence and temperance as virtues of character. There is certain idealism in being ethical. These are habits of the heart. Remember now that leaders are humans.

To put the question in a raw form: Can the exercise of influential power and idealism go together? I will not refer to local cases or to the Enron case, or the BP case, or to the banking crisis in the US. They make great case studies for this subject, but you would have heard of them, and I thought I should not replicate.

As I read out Percy Shelley's (1792–1822) Ozymandias, try and relate his poem to the subject of effective and ethical leadership.

I met a traveller from an antique land
Who said: "Two vast and trunkless legs
of stone
Stand in the desert. Near them, on the
sand,
Half sunk, a shattered visage lies, whose
frown,
And wrinkled lip, and sneer of cold
command,
Tell that its sculptor well those passions
read
Which yet survive, stamped on these
lifeless things,
The hand that mocked them and the
heart that fed:
And on the pedestal these words appear:
'My name is Ozymandias, king of kings:
Look on my works, ye Mighty, and
despair!'

Nothing beside remains. Round the decay
Of that colossal wreck, boundless and bare,
The lone and level sands stretch far away."

The next illustration is a familiar one: David and Goliath. David defeated Goliath and saved Israel, but later as king, he seduced Bathsheba and deliberately sent her husband to certain death in battle. That was effective but unethical.

Consider now the embryonic stem cell research. I chair the BAC [Bioethics Advisory Committee] now; I chaired the sub group that dealt with the ethical issues of this research. The contemporary issues then were with reproductive cloning, therapeutic cloning and regenerative medicine. The broader national context is this: Singapore wants to be among nations that are at the forefront of biomedical research but it must practice good science.

Embedded in this research is the moral status of the developing foetus. One view is that it is a person from the moment of conception, and therefore the research is wrong. But what if it involves the treatment of your very sick infant child? Another view is that the research can be for the common good in saving lives, healing diseases.

Conflicting? Can you mutually reinforce the progress of science and the ethics?

Consider another scenario. I am Singapore's Representative to the ASEAN Intergovernmental Commission on Human Rights. One issue is whether the exercise of human rights and freedoms "shall be subject … to such limitations as are determined by law … for the purpose of securing the recognition and respect for the rights and freedoms of others and of meeting the just requirements of morality, public order and general welfare…" Examples of the human rights are these:

All human beings are born free and equal in dignity and rights.

Everyone has the right to life, liberty and security of person.

All are equal before the law and are entitled without discrimination to equal protection of the law.

These are serious civil and political rights. In human rights discourse, these are first generation rights.

There are ten ASEAN nations involved. One school of thought is: you cannot take away fundamental human rights under any circumstances. We shall call this the first school of thought, just as a reference point for our discussion. The other school of thought is that the exercise of human rights, even fundamental freedoms, must be subordinated to certain prescribed state-sanctioned principles of public interest or the public good. We shall call this the second school of thought accordingly.

Underlying this debate is the organising principle of our society which is the primacy of the State, assuming, of course, the proper exercise of its powers. Would the first school of thought then dismantle this vital organising principle of our society? What weight do we then give to state sanctioned acts, in this case, qua human rights. That is at the macro level. At the practical level, if one needs to influence the first school of thought, would the ethical value of human flourishing which underlies fundamental freedoms be proscribed?

And while on the subject of state-sanctioned acts, we need to remember that Hitler's programs were state sanctioned too but we would say they were morally bad. Was he effective? Initially yes, but when he led his followers to disaster, that rendered him ineffective. In more contemporary times, so also was Saddam Hussein. Saddam Hussein effectively led Iraq to nationhood, but we would say that he was brutal and brought harm to his people. I was in the former Yugoslavia recently and heard from the officials of the stories of Slobodan Milosevic, who became the President of Serbia and then of the Federal Republic of Yugoslavia. He was tried at The Hague for war crimes, for his involvement in the Bosnian Genocide. He died in the course of his trial.

But where would you put Bill Clinton?

This would then lead me to the next matter: judging effectiveness and ethics in leadership.

Here I am guided by Joseph Nye, in his book, *The Powers to Lead*. He says this:

In practice, we can judge both effectiveness and ethics in three dimensions: goals, means and consequences. Effective goals combine realism and risk in a vision that can be implemented, whereas ethical goals are judged by the morality of the intentions and vision. Good goals have to meet our moral standards, as well as a feasibility test. Effective means are those that are efficient for achieving the goals, but ethical means depend on the quality, not the efficiency, of the approaches employed. A leader's consequential effectiveness involves achieving the group's goals, but ethical consequences means good results not just for the in-group, but for outsiders as well.

Let me relate Joseph Nye's clear analysis to the clearance of the backlog of a few thousand cases at the Subordinate Courts when I took office as the Senior District Judge in 1991. You have no

doubt heard of the aphorism: Justice delayed is justice denied.

The goal was to clear the backlog of cases, which had been in the Courts' dockets for some years. Remedies sought must be considered without undue haste; liberties of accused persons must be decided promptly. The ethical goals are certainly commendable if effective goals recognised the transactional realities of the processes; the various litigating parties, the public agencies.

The means to do this were to reallocate scarce resources, like night court, and interject headway processes, for example mediation, ensuring that these means are not hurried or speedy or basement justice, through established public protocols and amendments to Rule of Court. It was essential that Justice was done and seen to be done.

In a short period, the backlog of cases was cleared. Litigating parties had their day in court. Justice was administered in our society. Independent public surveys showed 95% confidence in our justice processes and system. The World Bank acknowledged our justice reforms as exemplary for developed and developing jurisdictions. That was a happy example, but not the next one. Leaders, to be effective, can be caught between a rock and a hard place, a dilemma.

Let me now discuss a conundrum on the ethical part of the equation. I am not personally in favour of gambling yet find myself as Chairman of the Casino Regulatory Authority. Can a leader maintain his conscience and sense of integrity by distinguishing between the public square and his private space? Joseph Nye pointed out that the 52nd Governor of New York, Mario Matthew Cuomo, was personally opposed to abortion as a Catholic, but argued that in his role as governor, he was obligated to think of the requirements of a public official in a pluralistic democracy. He kept the public and private spheres separate. Can you?

Michael Sandel in *What Money Can't Buy* tells this story. Barbara Harris is the founder of a North Carolina-based charity called Project Prevention, launched in 1997. Each year, hundreds of babies are born to drug-addicted mothers. Some of these babies are addicted to drugs, and a great many of them will suffer child abuse or neglect. Barbara Harris offers a market-based solution: offer drug-addicted women US$300 cash if they will undergo sterilisation or long-term birth control. More than 3,000 women have taken her up on the offer.

Critics call the project "morally reprehensible", a "bribe for sterilisation". The argument is that offering drug addicts a financial inducement to give up their reproductive capacity amounts to coercion, especially since the programme targets vulnerable women in poor neighbourhoods. Harris moralises that a woman's right to procreate is not more important than the right of a child to have a moral life. There seems here to be two equally compelling standards in the public square, and Barbara has decided to dirty her hands. "A dirty hand" is when leaders, in the interest of the group for whom they serve, may have to do things they would be unwilling to do in their private lives.

To apply this dilemma then to the Joseph Nye's three dimensions of goals, means and consequences, and to round up this part of the discussion. This is what he says:

"We tend to make moral judgments in terms of the three dimensions of goals, means, and consequences, often with a delicate weighing of the trade-offs among them. Because of their special roles, we often put more weight on consequences when judging leaders. At the same time, if followers allow leaders to argue that the duties of their roles require them to think only of consequences, they may slip into a self-justificatory style that too fully detaches them from other rules of moral behavior. Conscience and the search for a sense of personal integrity can be an important limit on the slippery slope of such overly permissive morality."

Are there no moral off limits, then?

In 2001, The New York Times published a story about a company in China that offers an unusual service: if you need to apologise to someone — an estranged lover or business partner with whom you've had a falling out — and you can't quite bring yourself to do so in person, you can hire the Tianjin Apology company to apologise on your behalf. The motto of the company is, "We say sorry for you." According to the article, the professional apologisers are "middle-aged men and women with

college degrees who dress in sombre suits. They are lawyers, social workers and teachers with "excellent verbal ability" and significant life experience, who are given additional training in counselling." Does a bought apology work? If someone wronged or offended you, and then sent a hired apologiser to make amends, would you be satisfied? It might depend on the circumstances, or perhaps even the cost. Would you consider an expensive apology more meaningful then a cheap one?

I have, out of respect for time, discussed the basic aspects of effective and ethical leadership. There is an added layer: I will mention this briefly to give us a glimpse into this universe, this "new normal" if you like.

More and more companies as well as public agencies involved in the delivery of services face adaptive challenges: these are changes in societies, markets, and technology which require their leaders to clarify values, develop new strategies, and learn new ways of operating. The challenge is this: leaders are accustomed to solving problems themselves. They now need to take on new roles, relationships, values, and approaches to work. Adaptive change is distressing and requires unlearning of historical practices and values, versus immutable values. The followers are

adapt to new challenges, are likely to face their own form of extinction.

Ronald Heifetz suggests some ways for leaders faced with an adaptive change. The details are perhaps for another occasion. Essentially, the adaptive demands of our time require leaders who take responsibility without waiting for revelation or request. One can lead with no more than a question in hand.

Essentially what I am saying is this: Leaders matter. Leadership matters. Leaders must be effective and ethical.

inclined towards being ambivalent about the sacrifices required of them and look to the leaders to shoulder the problems themselves.

Ronald Heifetz, lecturer at the John F. Kennedy School of Government, shares this illustration:

When a leopard threatens a band of chimpanzees, the leopard rarely succeeds in picking off a stray. Chimps know to respond to this kind of threat. But when a man with an automatic rifle comes near, the routine responses fail. Chimps risk extinction in a world of poachers unless they figure out how to disarm the new threat. Similarly, companies and public agencies which cannot learn quickly to

I will end with Invictus by William Ernest Henley:

Out of the night that covers me,
Black as the Pit from pole to pole,
I thank whatever gods may be
For my unconquerable soul.
In the fell clutch of circumstance
I have not winced nor cried aloud.
Under the bludgeonings of chance
My head is bloody, but unbowed.
Beyond this place of wrath and tears
Looms but the Horror of the shade,
And yet the menace of the years
Finds, and shall find, me unafraid.
It matters not how strait the gate,
How charged with punishments the scroll.
I am the master of my fate:
I am the captain of my soul.

Forum

Arnold Gay: How "dirty" are your hands? You're now the chairman of the Casino Regulatory Authority, after spending 40 years in the judiciary. How do you balance your personal views against the public good?

Richard Magnus: That's a very troubling question, it is a haunting question. How dirty are my hands? I try to understand what the issues are. I try to understand the rules of gaming. I try to understand the behaviour of potential gamblers. I try to understand the economic value of this. I try to understand the social repercussions of this particular area, so I dirty my hands trying to understand that and see what policies need to be put into place in order to proscribe the harm as much as possible and that's where the challenge really is.

I think fortunately we have fewer local citizens and permanent residents patronising the casinos. Remember the casinos were a political decision which we found ourselves in. But let me turn back the question to you, would you rather have someone who is unethical running the Casino Regulatory Authority? Would you rather have somebody else of a different shade, of a different inclination, running the Casino Regulatory Authority?

So I think it's a dilemma. I'm not saying I have solved the dilemma. It gives me nightmares from time to time when you read accounts of the consequences of gambling addiction and that's one of the reasons why I have quoted Joseph Nye, that whenever we judge this issue of effective leadership, we tend to look at consequences, and I think we need to sort of remember that there are other dimensions that are also involved in this particular area.

Audience: What is the best way to get the apathetic members of society involved in reaching the best decision possible? Assuming that one of the roles of effective leaders is to get consensus among everyone else, while at the same time without crossing the ethical clarity in coercing these apathetic members in society and persuading them.

Richard: That's a brilliant question. I think first, engagement is in fact a norm now. It has to be a norm. We can no longer go on the basis of making decisions autocratically without ensuring that you know really what their answers are, or say it is actually for their own good.

I think the issue is adaptive change or adaptive challenge, which I mentioned briefly in my speech. Engagement must become a norm. The question is whether they can reach a consensus in reality. Consensus means that everybody agrees and the only body that has decided on the norm of consensus is the European Union as well as ASEAN.

No other bodies have done it; in other words, it is not realistic within a society that is multi-cultural and multi-religious, and also cosmopolitan like Singapore to be able to arrive at a consensus. In other words, everyone agrees that this should be done, but everybody can agree, I think, with the ethics of it, with ethics of the decision that has been made and therefore, ethics would be the one that binds and unites the population, and there are quite a number of examples of this. Essentially that will be the reality of it.

Arnold: This was the issue as well at the town hall meetings you attended, where you described the settings and responses historically?

Richard: Without passing judgment on the constituency or the people attending those town hall meetings, I think their comments were sincere. They made those comments because they felt for their neighbourhoods, they felt for their families.

One of them said, "If you take away my void deck, where do my children play football and where can we get the wind in the evenings?" Of course, there are extremes to that, one chap said that if you do that you take away the *feng shui* in my house. I think they were quite sincere about that, though wrong, and it becomes an adaptive change, adaptive challenge. The question for the leaders, then, is really how to move in a different way in order to engage their concerns, sympathise, empathise with them, and try to work with them to arrive at a common solution.

The example that is given in the Kennedy school is this: if I were to go to a doctor and say to him I've got the flu, he will say take Panadol, so many times a day. If I go to the doctor and say I've got cancer, he'll say let's embark on a course of chemotherapy. But if I were to come to him and he is not able to diagnose my disease and I have to depend upon him for an answer, what do you do? So one solution that would be for the doctor to work with the patient and say, "I don't know what the problem is but I am prepared to walk with you in this particular phase of your life" and I think that is an adaptive change. There are no answers; we do not know what the answers are going to be, but it is the ability to walk that journey with the concerned.

Audience: During your time as a district judge, what is the most interesting case you saw, and how has it shaped you as a person today?

Richard: One case, I think, stands out even, as you ask this question. I had before me a man of the cloth, if you know what I mean, coming before me who was charged for cheating. Cheating is dishonesty.

Your first paradigm is to wonder how a man of the cloth could be dishonest; he is caught out for dishonesty. He makes dishonest statements and you begin to ask yourself as to what really happened to this man of the cloth. Where there is an entrustment, there is a dependence, and you actually go and share your life stories with them. This stands out, and I think it is important that although we do not formally say that we are in a position of authority, a position of power, we actually are.

In a very real sense, when we weigh a man of the cloth, there is a certain amount of respect; and if the respect is lost, then what is the value of the man?

Audience: Did you expect to achieve what you have so far?

Richard: It's interesting, our destiny sometimes takes a different turn and to expect to do all these things now, the answer is no. I would have known, of course, that I would go into the public service. I was in private practice and I did not find satisfaction, simply because I was working for money, for a client, whereas in public service I was working for the values of justice, right and wrong, to bring a certain sense of equilibrium. What the Bible calls respite — you do what is right, right what is wrong, you bring hope when there is despair, you bring peace where there is none.

Audience: You asked if we would rather be led by an unethical leader. So does it mean Christian values equate the right ethics, and non-Christian means unethical?

Also isn't it a little bit dogmatic or paternalistic for a certain group of people, for example Christians, to pose their ethic or morality onto another group? I ask this question with relation to Section 377A of the Penal Code.

Richard: Those are excellent questions. I am not equating being ethical to being Christian. I am not saying to be ethical is to be Christian.

[Part of the answer lies in] the contribution of Christianity or religion towards the morality of the state. I think it is a very existential question.

I did a study of this way back to the first century. It was an age called the Axial Age. In the Axial Age of civilisation you have got people like Laozi, Confucius, Buddha, altogether at the same time. It was also at the time when there was monotheism, belief in one God. And never in the history of civilisation has the Axial Age been duplicated, even till today. Some call it the Golden Age. It was from that age that the values began to seep down to the other subsidiary civilisations and to the other generations. So in fact today we say we have Confucian values, right? When did it happen? During the Axial Age. One of the Confucian values says that it is state first, individuals second. We have the values of Laozi, the sayings of Laozi,

for example, how you have personal integrity.

Aristotle and Laozi said almost the same thing: we need to have courage, you need to be bold and you need to face danger. Laozi in effect said that, so that was before Christ, it was in the BC era. Monotheism is found in the practice of various expressions of monotheism of various religions.

So the question is whether philosophy and religion have affected values, and the answer is yes. You don't have to look very far, you look at Singapore for example, you see the foundation of a lot of the values have seeped through all the various centuries. We passed common laws based on certain values.

You also ask whether only Christians have the exclusive right to say these are the right values. The answer is of course, no. I mentioned Laozi. I mentioned Confucius. I mentioned monotheistic beliefs and my expressions of that in society. For example, when I was in the AICHR, in the ASEAN, Intergovernmental Commission on Human Rights, I fought for the freedom of religion in ASEAN. And the reason why I fought for freedom of religion in ASEAN is because some countries in ASEAN have laws which say if you are of a certain religion, it becomes a criminal

offence. So with regards to freedom of religion, I am not only saying freedom of expression of Christianity, but freedom of religion. Because I think that the free expression of religion is important.

Audience: Do leaders need to learn soft skills like philosophy more than technical skills, so they can better understand issues like morality and human rights? Would it help reduce the abuse of power?

Richard: Leaders exercise what has been called hard power and soft power. Hard power is when I am making the strategic decisions — these

are my plans. These are my timelines. These are what I evaluate with. I draw a distinction with output and outcome for example. These are hard power decisions.

But leaders also need to have soft power. How would you culturalise a company? What's the DNA of your company? How would you motivate your pupils?

This is the soft power part and ethics is a large part of the soft power exercised by leaders.

Do the leaders need to learn? I think not formally. You don't have to be a leader and say I did philosophy, et cetera; and if you look at our broad leadership in Singapore, these are skills that need to be learnt.

Leadership is not born, it is learnt. I think we need to recognise that. So my thesis is that ethics is such an important core of a leader's life, for the corporation that he is in, the public agency that he is in, to be sustainable.

In other words he defines the DNA of his followers, of this company, or his public agency.

Some of these rights are basic to us. From young we are taught about right and wrong, proper and improper action. So some of these things are already embedded within our DNA, and it's recognising and expressing this particular aspect of our DNA as leaders that becomes quite important.

Audience: As a man of ethics, when it comes to a question of science and ethics, would you say it's ever justifiable to compromise in the realm of ethics for the science of development, like the Nazis did during World War II?

Arnold: I don't think we even have to go back that far, right? You're dealing with this in your role as ethics advisor.

Richard: There is the issue of embryonic stem cell. Embryonic stem cells are derived from a baby when conceived, and you take out the DNA from the baby and then with the DNA from the baby you begin to develop a liver for example, or you develop a heart, or you develop a kidney and when the baby is unwell, then when the baby is suffering from kidney or liver damage, which is quite fatal, you take this stem cell which has been shaped and alive and you put it back into the baby and it will heal the baby. That's a possible science, that has been done and Singapore has got expertise in the area; 16 patents in this area belong to Singapore. In the world, I think there are 29 patents, and 16 belong to Singaporeans.

So the issue is what is the value that you place on the baby? Is the baby alive, is the baby a person? Can you intervene with the baby's life? Can you change the DNA of the baby? Would you want to change the DNA of the baby? What is the meaning of life, that kind of thing? So when does life form? So when you reduce it the basic question is "when is life formed?" One school says, that is at the time of conception, once the sperm fertilises the egg, that's life, it becomes alive. If that is correct, then you don't intervene with the baby. But the question I ask is, "What if it was

Mr Richard R Mag...
...PPA(E) (L)
Chai... ...o Regulatory A...

your baby and you know that the baby may die if the liver is not therapeutically managed?" What would you do then?

If you have the conception that life begins at that point, there would be tension with regard to this particular area. You would have read the book by Jodi Picoult. Jodi Picoult has written a book, *My Sister's Keeper*. The story is about parents who have a daughter and the girl is suffering from several diseases, fatal diseases, and they were trying to use the parents' tissues but there was a lot of rejection. The doctors, the specialists tell them the only way to be able to save your girl is to have another child and you take the tissue from that child which is more compatible. So the parents decide to give birth to another child so they could save the older child. There was a motivation. The question is whether it is the right motivation or the wrong motivation. That's one issue. Would you raise a child up to a certain age, it came to a stage, where every month the elder sister and this young little baby would go and there was an exchange of tissue and it goes on until they were teenagers. The question is what happens when the younger girl realises that she has been born for the purpose of therapy for the sister. So again, the value of life — what would you do in that particular case? So there is a tension in this area.

Audience: Would you not agree that ethics is a matter based highly on perspective? Dr Fritz Haber invented the ammonia process which sustains billions of lives in Asia today through his fertiliser, yet he is also the man who convinced the German Army to gas the Allies.

Richard: I think Nazi Germany was a morally bad regime, they don't even respect the victims as human beings, they equate them with animals so that's a different perspective altogether. Recognising someone as a person means this person has got the dignity, it means this person has life, it means this

person has got certain rights and that's the basic thing.

But let me tell you how we resolved the dilemma for the embryonic stem cells issue. Number one, we said that there should not be any reproductive cloning. We cannot make another person; we cannot have a Jodi Picoult example. We could not have another used teddy bear, a better you; all your diseases we take out and there's a better you, that is out of the question, that is not what life is all about right? So that choice is out. Reproductive cloning, they gave in with Dolly the sheep, she carried on and everybody was quite happy with Dolly the sheep until Dolly was 5 years old and began to exhibit very unusual diseases and then died. So we don't know what is going to happen with cloning.

But in terms of therapeutic care, remember the example of taking the DNA and putting it back into the baby? The way we resolved it was to leave the choice to the parents. You conscience is therefore not affected. It is your freedom; it is not by state mandate. It is by your freedom which you have in the first place. So that choice is preserved; so far as you are concerned, ethics have not been broken. I recognise your ethics. I recognise that there is also this progress of science, but you make the final decision. Not the state, you decide. Would you allow your infant baby to die? You make that decision. That is the ethics part of it.

Arnold: Tell me a little bit about this outlook of wanting to serve. You could have been a CEO of a multinational company, yet you have chosen largely to serve the public.

Richard: Interestingly, I've been Chairman. I've seen the various sides, so when I talk about effectiveness and leadership, I'm also thinking within the corporate context. But the common bond is that it is the person that moves across.

Your ethics follow you, so to speak. And I think if there is awareness that ethics is

critical, ethics is essential, then it follows you wherever you go. In other words, will you be able to make a difference in your setting? How different are you in your setting from another person? And I am putting forward a thesis that having ethics would enable you to make that difference.

Audience: Has there been a leadership moment in your career which has helped shaped you?

Richard: I remember I was quite happily working in the Ministry of Defence; I was in government linked companies. But when I was with the court suddenly I began to realise that this was a different paradigm altogether.

I remember the first day that I went to court, I remember I went to the bench and I had to hear a criminal case, had to decide whether this person is guilty or not and being vested with the power to send him to prison. That was a difficult moment when I found the person guilty and sent him to prison. I called the lawyer to my chambers and told him: "Please appeal against my decision." Would a judge ever ask that? But I recognised that this was a moment in which I needed to be confident and responsible to the public trust that was entrusted to me, one person who is called a judge on the bench. With powers to incarcerate, with powers to send people to prison, with powers to set people free, with regard to that.

So rights were involved, people were involved, principles were involved, the rights of the person affected, the family members who were in court at the time. And that was the moment that etched in my mind and the significance of the power that is given to us. It is a formal power but the exercise of the power is of much virtue. It continues to be so.

Tony Chew

Chairman
Singapore Business Federation

Tony Chew (SJI Alumnus 1965) is Executive Chairman of Asia Resource Corporation which has diversified business interests in the region. He is also Chairman of KFC Vietnam Company, Chairman of Macondray Corporation Pte Ltd and an Independent Director of Keppel Corporation.

He has been instrumental in many start-ups. Corporations include Jetstar Asia, Pepsi-Cola Vietnam, KFC Vietnam and International Beverages Myanmar, while government initiatives include Duke-NUS Graduate Medical School, Network Indonesia, Vietnam Business Club, Singapore Business Federation (SBF) and the ASEAN Business Advisory Council. He is also credited with the turnaround of several established companies such as Del Monte Pacific, Pepsi-Cola Bottler and Rothmans, in the Philippines.

In Singapore, he plays an active role in promoting regional businesses, having served on the Trade Development Board, Regional Business Forum, Economic Review Sub-Committee for

Entrepreneurship and Internationalisation (2001/2002), GPC Resource Panel for Finance, Trade and Industry, Chairman of Network Indonesia as well as Vietnam Business Club, and Member of ASEAN Business Advisory Council. He was also a Member of the Economic Strategies Committee (2009/2010).

He is presently Chairman of Singapore Business Federation, Chairman of Duke-NUS Graduate Medical School Singapore, and Member of the Economic Research Institute for ASEAN and East Asia Governing Board, Chinese Development Assistance Council Board of Trustees, National Productivity and Continuing Education Council, and Advisor to Singapore Institute of International Affairs. He was conferred the Public Service Medal in 2001, Public Service Star in 2008 and NUS Outstanding Service Award 2011.

Dr Koh Thiam Seng, SJI Principal, Vincent Anandraj, Chairman, organising committee and Mr Arnold Gay, moderator for today, parents of SJI, good afternoon.

It is my honour to deliver the Fullerton-SJI leadership lecture. I never thought of myself as a leader, and was quite anxious about giving a lecture on leadership. I spent some time penning a speech about my life journey. After a few efforts, I realised I am no autobiographer. But I have some points to share about my life, which I hope you will find interesting and helpful.

Let me open with a quote from Henry Kissinger, the noted statesman.

"The task of the leader is to get his people from where they are to where they have not been."

"From where they are", where was I in my early years? I was very poor and very humble. My father was a small-time contractor and my mother worked as a housekeeper to feed nine children. When I was in Primary Six, I was so malnourished that the principal (Brother Gabriel) gave me a bottle of milk each day and made me drink it in front of him. Perhaps he felt that if I didn't drink

it, I may have brought it home to share with my eight siblings. Those days, we always shared what little food we had.

It has been a long journey from that point, in the principal's office drinking free milk, to now. Looking at my CV, I myself am shocked — chairman of my own companies, Chairman of the Singapore Business Federation, and Chairman of Duke-NUS Graduate Medical School. Sometimes I still have to glance at the photo to check, if this is indeed me. If it is, then how did I get here?

There were three factors in my journey:

First of all, I had a plan, a target, a vision, or perhaps just a dream. Secondly, I didn't do it alone. I had mentors, partners and colleagues, some of whom are here today. Thirdly, I had a strong sense of commitment.

In 1960, when I was in Secondary One, I was accepted into the household of a prominent businessman and lived with his family for five years. He would talk to his sons over dinner about his extensive businesses in Singapore, Malaysia and Hong Kong. He did not know it, in fact he hardly talked to me, but I was in the background, listening intently to his every word.

This man, Mr Ko Teck Kin, was an inspiration to me. He never went past primary school. He spoke no English. Self-taught, he developed business skills and made a wide network of business connections. He was one of the most successful businessmen of his day. Not only was he a successful businessman, but he also devoted time and wealth to the community; co-founding the Nanyang University and putting up the Chinese Chamber of Commerce building when he was its chairman. He also became our first High Commissioner to Malaysia. I particularly remember how his views were sought by political leaders and prime ministers of both Singapore and Malaysia, who came to his house to consult him. I remember being rushed out of the dining room one evening because of a special visitor. He was none other than Mr Lee Kuan Yew.

Mr Ko gave me a vision, and an inspiration. I saw in him the success, the public service, and the wisdom which I hoped for, from that day till now.

And he taught me humility. Although I lived in the house, I was not part of the family. I was an outsider, listening in. I was on my own.

I had no choice about my first job. Ko Teck Kin died young, at age 55. I was sent, like others in the Ko household to run his rubber estates in Malaysia. This career did not last long, Singapore left Malaysia in 1965, and in 1969 racial riots broke out in Malaysia and I considered leaving that country.

Singapore was small, poor and in a war-torn region. Malaysia had kicked us out, Indonesia was fighting us. Much of Singapore was a shanty town, Jurong was still a swampland. Many of my friends had emigrated.

A former classmate invited me to his home for dinner one evening. During dinner, his father, a qualified engineer working in the Public Works Department, told us they were migrating to the UK. Why? "Singapore will not be able to sustain itself," he said. The Mandarin Hotel (which was being built then) would consume more electricity than a small Malaysian town. How was Singapore going to pay for its electricity?

When my friends were leaving Singapore, I made a decision to return to Singapore. It was a commitment to stay and work, and make my life in Singapore. And perhaps one day to build my own business.

I had to learn new business skills. I could not afford to go to business school, so I created my own "business school." I joined Guthrie's, a large British trading firm, to learn about marketing, sales and trading. Two years later I joined an Indonesian family business, the Sampoerna Group, to learn about Indonesia, the people and its markets. In those five years I learnt as much as I could, observing, listening and studying the different people, their business cultures, and management styles.

When I could, I took up simple training courses, like learning how to type and accounting. Later, when I could afford them, I attended executive programs, including those in INSEAD and Harvard. I also joined business Organisations like YPO (Young Presidents' Organization), and attended conferences such as the World Economic Forum in Davos.

I was always preparing myself for opportunities that may come my way. I met an entrepreneur Ted de Ponti, who was originally from Holland, and 20 years older than me. He was former head of Philip Morris Indonesia, with vast knowledge and experience in the country. In 1974, he invited me to be his business partner, and I accepted.

Working with Ted was an education in business for me. I learnt the importance of "trust" in business. I learnt how to build "trust" by being correct, careful, honest, punctual and meticulous in every part of business. If you are trustworthy, your customers will buy from you, your suppliers will support you, the banks will give you credit.

We were a small trading company — we didn't have much capital. Trust was our capital.

With our reputation of integrity and trustworthiness, we made good progress, especially in Indonesia. In 1979 we secured our first big deal, and made over a million dollars profit that year. It was a lot of money in those days, and we could have retired comfortably. Instead, we reinvested all of it in the company, hiring people and investing in new businesses.

Our strategy was to focus on emerging, underdeveloped countries where competition was less fierce. Not many companies ventured into these difficult markets which were very risky, both financially and in terms of safety.

I remember the many times I came close to death, while conducting my business, on the road. Our ventures were in countries that were war-torn and unstable. On one occasion I was held in a Manila hotel for three days as it had been overrun by rebels and surrounded by soldiers and tanks. In Jakarta, I had a lucky

escape from a racial riot — where the hotel's ground floor lobby was totally destroyed. In Tehran I was prevented from leaving the country for a few days. And in Myanmar I had to drive 16 hours overnight from Mandalay to Yangon, on dirt roads where rebels were active. I was lucky to survive those close calls.

Another skill I had to learn was to seek out local partners in each country that we invested in. The choice of the right business partner is the most fateful decision in an overseas venture. With the correct partner, the investment process, although still difficult, is much smoother. With the wrong partner, you waste valuable time and opportunities. Those with the right partnerships will soon overtake you.

We were fortunate to find excellent and trustworthy partners who are still our partners and friends till this day. It took ten years to build our business.

In 1986 when our trading business was more stable, we decided to diversify and invest in large companies with established international brands. Our first major acquisitions were Pepsi-Cola, Rothmans and Del Monte in the Philippines. This was yet another chapter in my life. I needed a new skill set.

Large corporations with thousands of employees are run by business systems and processes beyond the individuals. Yet trust, honesty, integrity and meticulousness are as important with a large corporation as when I ran a small trading company. I had to learn about systems, processes and controls, about boards of directors, corporate governance and financial audits. Without them, the company can collapse, however good its business.

Another skill I had to learn was to develop good working relationships at the government level. Understanding the regulatory environment, safety, taxation and investment controls are crucial. I learnt to work closely with governments and authorities of the countries which I invested in. This was a very special skill.

Subsequently I embarked on many new start-ups — Pepsi-Cola Vietnam, KFC Vietnam, International Beverages Myanmar, Jetstar Asia, altogether over 20 new ventures. I also invested in, and turned around a number of older companies, including Pepsi-Cola Philippines, Del Monte Philippines, Myanmar Airways International, Hangzhou Hua Feng Paper Mill, etc.

In 1990 I turned another chapter of my life — that of Public Service. That year, my partner and mentor of 16 years, Ted de Ponti, died. He was an exceptional person. Not only was he an excellent businessman, he also devoted time for his friends and his charity work. Hundreds of boys and girls benefited from his generosity, through scholarships, books and medical treatment. When he died, Ngee Ann Polytechnic commissioned a book *Give with the Heart* to recognise him.

His death sparked memories of Mr Ko and his record of public service that inspired me to start my own career of public service. That year, I made a commitment to look beyond my business and to dedicate myself to Singapore.

My public service was based on my business, investment skills and my knowledge. In 1991, I served on the Regional Business Forum, co-chaired by the Ministry of Trade and Industry (MTI) and the Ministry of Finance (MOF). This was followed by other invitations to serve on other government and economic agency initiatives. In the past 20 years, I must have chaired or served on at least 20 committees, boards and councils; the most significant being the Trade Development Board, Singapore Business Federation, Vietnam Business Club and Network Indonesia.

This taught me yet another skill: to bring together many partners, from all over the world and get them to work together effectively. This was key when I was invited to chair the governing board of Duke-NUS Graduate Medical School in 2005.

I have learnt much from my public service work. I learned about government policies, and how our government and civil service run the country. This has helped me understand and bridge issues by bringing business and government together on problems and seek solutions. I also ventured into areas well outside my normal domain, working with a wide diversity of outstanding medical and academic leaders in the Duke-NUS Graduate Medical School. This has been my education, and my great satisfaction, in my later life.

People have asked me if I was lucky. My view is that many people have good luck but don't make use of it. Others have bad luck, but manage to overcome it. I didn't have that much luck myself; in fact, I had a terrible start in life and many difficulties along the way.

Instead of luck, I had three factors: commitment, a plan, and a lot of help from others.

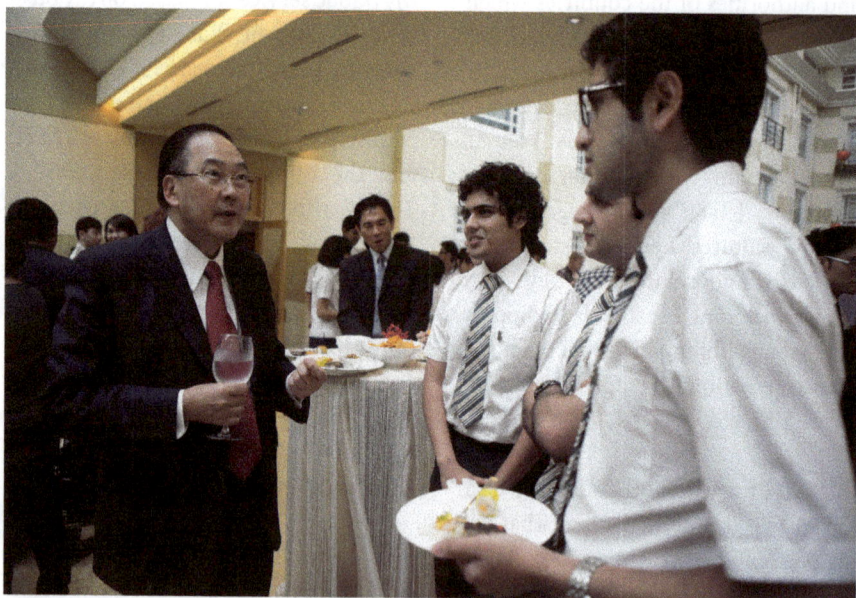

I committed myself at a young age to be a successful businessman, run my own company, and to be of service to the community. From that point on, I started to plan, to acquire skills, and to muster the resources. This plan allowed me to be at the right place, the right time, and with the right skills and resources, to finally start my own business. This was much more important than "luck."

Then, my life helpers: mentors who inspired and taught me, partners in many countries who helped me start my overseas ventures, and a strong team of young colleagues, some of whom are here today. They believed in my plan, shared my vision and my hopes for the future. They all played a critical part in my life's journey. Without them, I would not be here today.

Lastly, I made a commitment to Singapore. This was my life's most fateful decision. Once I made this decision, it set my direction; it gave me a strong compass by which I made all my subsequent decisions. Otherwise I may not have planned well. I may not have been able to achieve my goals. And I could not have made the long journey from my secondary school days in SJI, drinking free milk, to speaking with you today. I will be happy to take your questions. Thank you.

Forum

Audience: You speak very much about your business enterprises and how you've progressed through life really against the flow and really making yourself as great as you can be but I want to ask is: "what was your motivation to go as far as you did?" Was it success, was it independence? What was that factor that drove you to get to where you are?

Tony Chew: Initially it was about survival and sustaining myself. Later, it was about being successful in my ventures and to be independent. I come from a different era, a time in Singapore when poverty, deprivation and unemployment were widespread, and communist threat and racial riots were very real, something you don't see today. It was not easy to get a job then, some even stooped to begging. I was fortunate to become a plantation manager in Malaysia, which was a good job in those days. In 1970, following the racial riots in Malaysia, I was compelled to return to Singapore. So I had to start over again, to learn new skills, understand new markets and develop a new career path. I joined Guthrie's, a large British trading house, followed by the Sampoerna Group, an Indonesian family business. When I joined them I had to learn as much as I could about marketing, sales, and trading, knowing that one day I could use these skills to be in business of my own and be my own boss. When Ted de Ponti invited me to be his business partner in 1974, I accepted without hesitation because I felt I was ready and that I could contribute to the venture.

Arnold Gay: I want to ask, and maybe some of the younger members of the audience might want to ask this as well: can you do anything for fun anymore? Can you still do something like run a business and make it a success and not so much because you have to survive?

Tony: Actually running a successful business takes more than fun. The environment is very competitive, and the venture must be profit motivated in order to sustain itself. A few of my young executives are here. In Indo-China we have a number of companies. James over there sits on the board of KFC Vietnam. He's doing great as he grew a small business into a vibrant company that now employs over four thousand people. James, I'm sure, is having some fun although there are also challenges. We also have Charlie who focuses on our Myanmar ventures, and Alvin is looking after the medical device related business. They choose their areas of interest, and if I think that it is an opportunity to support them, why not? In SBF which I chair, we formed the mentorship programme for promising entrepreneurs where we invite experienced businessmen in their 50s to 70s to act as mentors for the young mentees. These mentors are prepared to devote time and attention to coach our promising young SME entrepreneurs.

Audience: In this era, assuming you're a 16-year-old now, what course would you take in order to be successful? We know that it's going to be very competitive going forward. Also you're a pioneer in Myanmar, a developing country that's opening up and offering lots of potential. What advice would you give fellow Singaporeans who wish to start up something there?

Tony: Things have changed so much today, with so many opportunities compared to when I was 16. I had wanted to be a lawyer when I was young, which would have been a big mistake. In my business today I engage top lawyers who are so outstanding that I realise I might have been only a very average lawyer. Scanning the job market today, I would probably take up an engineering programme because there is such a high demand for engineers. I understand the number of students choosing engineering course have dropped and even those graduating as engineers have migrated to non-engineering jobs. In the Duke-NUS Graduate Medical School, one of the biggest groups of students comes from engineering backgrounds. I think there are lots of opportunities for those taking up engineering.

Regarding Myanmar, I have been in business there for almost 20 years. We have a strong presence there, employing about 3,000 people. We started the venture back in 1996 together with Seagram, a US MNC, to put up an alcoholic beverages business. But just before the equipment arrived, they decided to pull out of the venture, citing human rights issues. So they did not contribute their capital, their brands and their management know-how as agreed. It was a great shock to our local partner, a young Myanmar engineer, who had modest resource.

We decided to support him and continued with the project even though the risks were high, and appointed him as Managing Director. We funded the project, assembled a management team, learnt the technology and business, developed our own brands, and built nation-wide distribution. It was one of our best decisions. Today, after 16 years we have 70% market share of standard whiskey, 60% of gin and 20% of rum, and are very profitable. More importantly, we groomed a young local role model, who is today recognised by his peers as a self-made businessman, active in CSR activities.

Whether it is in Myanmar, Vietnam or China, there will be opportunities, challenges and risks. In Myanmar, foreigners are restricted from some businesses, including trading, retail, mining, etc. It is important to choose our local partners wisely, start with manageable scale and affordable risk, and expand when we understand the environment better and are more comfortable with the risks.

Audience: What do you think is the most important value a leader should possess in order to succeed?

Tony: As mentioned in my speech, although I assumed responsibilities, I did not seek to be a leader, nor saw myself as one. But one thing we should always do is to conduct ourselves well, maintain a high level of integrity, deliver on our commitments, excel in what we do, and lead by example.

Before coming to this lecture, I looked through an old school photo album, and realised that I took on several responsibilities in my Pre-U years in SJI. These included being president of the Geography Society, History Society, vice-president of the LDDS, and business manager for the 1964 school play at the Victoria Theatre called "Arsenic and Old Lace", which had to be stopped halfway on its opening night due to racial riots that broke out at the Padang.

Audience: What about new entrepreneurs and new businessmen? What is the most important characteristic or quality they must have when venturing out into a new world?

Tony: Management style today is certainly different from my time. For example, our superiors used to "direct" us without being questioned, but today we need to "engage" our team members. But in terms of leadership style, I believe everybody has a different style. I am very tough on my team members in terms of achieving desired outcomes. It is important to have clear targets otherwise we may be doing a lot of things without accomplishing our objectives.

At the same time, I try to lead by example. If I am not prepared to do something, then, how can I ask someone else to do it? Also, when we succeed we must give recognition to the whole team, and not try to claim credit for ourselves, leaving the rest behind. So I think different people have different ways of leading.

Audience: How can young people aspire to a life of business and enterprise and move beyond looking for a cushy job, and wanting to just climb the corporate ladder?

Tony: Commitment is important; the difference during my era and today is such that during my time we were faced with different kinds of difficulties. It was about survival, about taking risks, it was also about wanting to succeed. You don't want to fail. When we first started our business we had very little capital. With our limited resources we did not want to be competing with the big companies. So we had to seek our own market niches, starting with Indonesia, followed by Philippines, Vietnam, Myanmar, China. So that's what we did.

I agree with you, and hope that the youth today will look beyond immediate personal comfort but seek opportunities with some risks too. You're living in a different world from my time. You're in the Internet age where information is at your fingertips. During my time, we didn't even have a phone at home. I remember working in Malaysia where each minute of phone call from Johor to Singapore was expensive. At about 50 cents per minute, so you restrict your calls to a few minutes.

There must be this desire at an early age to be different, and to recognise, create or seize the opportunities that come your way. There will always be opportunities, but you need to be observant. When you are observant you see a lot more things than those who are not, and are better able to anticipate and plan.

Audience: How do you find and how do you identify a good partner? Is it by chance, or do you have to find and look through your sources?

Tony: Finding the right partner is so important, including your spouse. I tell you, don't take that lightly because you know, I have been very fortunate as my wife has been invaluable, in my business and my family and so on. So how did I find these persons? You have to devote time, and meet people, in order to seek them out. With trials or a cold call? I hired an overseas Vietnamese as my manager for Vietnam in 1991. He was

trained as an engineer, and was married to a Singaporean. He was prepared to spend a lot of time in Vietnam, and he identified a number of people for me, including Mr Trai who became my partner for Pepsi Vietnam, and Mr Kien who is our partner for KFC Vietnam.

Audience: I just graduated from SJI International and I am interested in developmental economics so I was quite interested in your opinion on investing in developing economies. Why did you invest in these precariously developing economies?

Tony: We were still a very small company then. And that would be the most expeditious route in terms of the opportunities, and costs of entry into those markets. Also, I felt that I could work better with the people than if they were large multinationals. I also felt that the playing field was a little more even for us.

Audience: In my school, we have this saying: "you don't have to be a perfect leader; you just have to be a passionate pioneer." Can passion sustain success?

Tony: Passion is important, but you have to cap it with reality. Most of my work has been in the pioneering areas, in my business as well as my public service. When Singapore started the Duke-NUS Graduate Medical School in 2005 I was invited to chair the governing board. It was a difficult decision for me. My background was agriculture, how was I going to lead a group of global academic and medical leaders?

But we need to feel confident in order to plan and execute well. Duke-NUS was a significant investment, focusing in two areas; medical education and medical research. We were introducing into Singapore for the first time the US MD graduate-entry medical education system. So we recruited top talent in terms of faculty and students, to ensure that our end product — the clinician scientist — will be of high quality. With a strong management team and an outstanding governing board, we managed to accomplish Duke-NUS' objectives.

Another example was Singapore's first business network. Called the "Vietnam Business Club", it was initiated by EDB in 1994, and I was invited as the inaugural chairman. EDB's objective was to encourage Singapore companies to invest in Vietnam, which was a promising emerging market. We had excellent people in the council — Lim Chee Oon, Wee Ee Cheong, Chong Quee Wah, and other senior business leaders. Within two and half years, Singapore rose from being 11th largest foreign direct investor in Vietnam to the number 1 position. The quality of the Secretariat team contributed to the success. Today, of the two young secretariat members, one is deputy CEO in a large GLC, and the other a senior government officer.

Other government initiatives that I was invited to serve on included Network Indonesia in 2002 and SBF Council that same year. These were all pioneering projects, so we must commit time and effort for them to succeed.

Audience: Do you have any failures and how do you cope with failure?

Tony: Actually I didn't only have successes, but also many failures and one good example is Macondray Packaging Pte Ltd. We invested $15 million into the project just before the Asian Financial Crisis in 1997, but the business did not survive even one year as we had not planned for contingencies. We have to just pick ourselves up and learn from our failures. Then it is not totally

wasted. Even in failures we can extract value if we can draw lessons from them.

Audience: If you were given a second chance to do something, what would you like to improve and why?

Tony: That's a fitting question to close this session. You know I went through a lot of highs and lows. But I don't think there's anything that I would like to change. I did go through a number of traumatic experiences, but also managed to get myself out of the crises. It's when you manage to get yourself out of serious trouble that you become more resilient, and be able to avoid similar problems or get out of them again the next time around. If I were to change that, then I might also miss the opportunities which followed. So it's better to take the blows, good and bad.

Today, I'm a lot older than you; I'm looking at other areas of importance beyond just growing businesses. Is there anything I would like to change? I don't think so! If I were to change anything it might impact the overall result. I don't think where I am today is too bad; I enjoy doing what I'm doing, especially in serving the community because at the end of the day it's not just our individual company or ourselves that counts, but it's the business community and also the broader community.

Jeremy Monteiro

Musician, Composer

Jeremy Monteiro, Jazz Pianist/Composer/Crooner/Educator (SJI Alumnus 1976), is regarded as Singapore's "King of Swing" by the Singaporean, Malaysian, Thai and Japanese press. Jeremy has released over 20 Jazz albums and played on numerous albums of other Jazz artists, including one by Grammy Award-winning Jazz saxophonist Ernie Watts which Jeremy also produced.

He has since been featured in over 400 published press articles at home and internationally. Jeremy is Visiting Chair of Jazz and Professor at LASALLE College of the Arts in Singapore and a Fellow of the London College of Music;

a part of University of West London, UK. In addition, Jeremy is a Fellow of the Royal Society for the encouragement of the Arts, Manufactures and Commerce (The RSA) in the UK, which is under the Patronage of the Queen of England. Some past Fellows of the RSA are Benjamin Franklin, Charles Dickens and Nelson Mandela while current Fellows include Prof Stephen Hawking.

Jeremy was the first pianist and Jazz musician to receive Singapore's pinnacle award in Arts Achievement — the Cultural Medallion. He was a Council Member of the National Arts Council from 2006 to 2010.

Thank you very much for the kind introduction, and also for the great music from William and Benjamin, thank you, well played. I asked for this lecture to be more in a question-and-answer format, I'm sorry I'm not really a very good orator, but I said that I would give an introduction, a little bit about my life as a musician growing up.

I actually started off very young; my father was a part-time Jazz guitarist and Hawaiian guitarist while also being a bass man. And he used to have Jazz sessions in his house and the early '60s and very often during the breaks I would jump up onto the piano or the organ that was there and fool around and start playing and my father's friend told him, "Monty, you better sell this lousy organ and get a proper piano for your son to take some piano lessons." And so he did when I was 5 years old. My father bought a quite inexpensive China-made piano called a "Blessing" piano. And I started learning the piano and it turned out to be quite a blessing for me because I think if I was not a musician today, I'm not sure what I would do.

I started learning the piano and at first I really loved my lessons. I started at the age of 6. But after a while, after quite a few whackings on my wrist with a ruler by the piano teacher, I really started to dislike my lessons. And I remember at the age of 9, at being forced to practise again I really felt that I didn't want to practise anymore. We were living in Sabah, in Kota Kinabalu at the time and my father had a small, sort of dwarf motorcycle, with very small wheels, but it was a real motorcycle and I went outside and started the engine and got the engine very, very hot to a point where it was, you know, the engine was just running and I, on purpose, put my leg against the engine to burn my leg so I won't have to [practise playing the piano]. I was learning to use the pedal at the time, the sustain pedal.

So I cried running into the house and I said, "Mum, I can't practise because I burnt my leg on the motorcycle." And my mother says, "Oh, you silly boy!" And she puts, you know the old wives' tale, she puts some butter on my leg and she says, "Is that feeling much better now?" I say, "Yeah, I'm feeling much better now." And she says; "Okay, now you go and practise but you don't have to press the pedal."

But I was very lucky because living in Sabah, Kota Kinabalu, was a fully-trained piano teacher by the name of Mr Tan Tze Tong. To have a trained piano teacher like Mr Tan teach me changed my life. Mr Tan was one of the earliest

Master's Degree holders in piano performance in Southeast Asia. And he actually was the first piano teacher who could actually demonstrate every single thing that he was teaching.

With music and art I think very often, those who know, do; those who don't, teach. But I'm sure that's not the case now with our teachers, but back in the day, it happened often. I mean, in the arts really, if your teacher can't show you what is it that he's trying to explain to you in words with a proper demonstration. It doesn't really impress upon the student.

Mr Tan could demonstrate not only the finer points about the technical things about music, but he could also demonstrate to me. If you talked about emotion, he could play one version which is perfectly correct technically speaking, but devoid of emotion and then do the same piece again for me fully infused with emotion and I think the ability to show me how to do it was a turning point for me and I fell in love with music again.

So this went on for a couple of years when I lived in Sabah; when I came over to Singapore I continued with other teachers but he had already ignited my love and my passion for music. And I continued, I only actually officially studied up to Grade 7 of the Royal School of Music, I actually learnt and prepared my pieces but I was a bit upset at that

time that the Royal School of Music had not changed for 80 to 90 years and as a 15 to 16 year-old boy, my protest was to not take the Grade 8 exam. At the age of 16 and a half I finished my 'O' levels at SJI.

I did very well in primary school in De La Salle but when I got to secondary school I found that I wasn't that interested in my studies. But in Sec 2, I was in a class where I felt very inspired to do well and I had great teachers who basically got me to become a good student and I passed so well that I got into what I think is the best Sec 3 class at the time, 3 Science 7, although some people at the time would have said that 3 Science 5 or 3 Science 6 was better. Unfortunately when I had got to Sec 3 I had lost my interest in studies as I was so fully into music at the time and I think I was the worst student in the best class of the school. And I think it's better to be the best student in the worst class. When I was in Secondary 1, I was very fortunate because I met someone who was a year older than me, a gentleman by the name of Hilarion Goh and he actually lived next door to the old SJI on Queen Street and in the living room of his house he had a nice piano, an organ and a drum set. And so the three of us, Hilarion, another musician from SJI, Ricky Ho, and myself would cross the road after school, and instead of going home, we would go to his house to have Jazz sessions until late in the afternoon, alternating between drums, organ and piano; so we would rotate and play all the instruments all afternoon. Also next door to the old SJI was City Music, the piano shop as well as the music shop and they had organs there as well; organs and pianos. And the owner Willy Hoe decided that he would guide me and give me some lessons whenever I was in his shop and he was in the mood. He actually taught me the differentiation between playing an acoustic piano and an electric piano and the organ, the Hammond organ, and those were invaluable lessons that remain with me till today.

I had already decided when I was 15 years old that I wanted to become a professional musician, particularly in the world of Jazz. When I was 16 and a half years old, in 1977, after I finished 'O' levels, which I just scraped through, I was very lucky because my mum, who was a private nurse, had nursed this owner of a Jazz club after his heart operation and during the time she was taking care of him. That was Mr A.J Isaac. He asked my mum, "What does your son do?" And she said, "Well he plays Jazz piano." So he says, "Well when I am better I'd like for you to bring him to an audition to the Club 392, on Orchard Road."

So I went for the audition and I was very lucky at that age to not only get the job as the pianist for the Club 392 but also as the band leader, which was very rough because at 16 and a half years old, with the other musicians in their 30s and 40s, it's not so easy to do. There was this occasion when one of my musicians wanted to beat me up because I told him to stop coming late to work. It was not easy to do but still it was a wonderful experience.

Soon after, someone else joined the band, a great guitar player who recently passed away by the name of Martin Pereira. He invited me to play at EMI Records for a couple of records for Matthew and the Mandarins and Frances Yip. Then they actually hired me as a full-time musician for EMI Records and in the '70s at the tender age of 17, I had a chance to play on more than 200 pop records in addition to having a career as a Jazz pianist. Just before I went into the army I was also asked by Warner Music to produce an album for Rahimah Rahim, a wonderful pop singer in the '70s, who is still very active today. I became the youngest Warner Brothers associate music producer in the world ever. So that was a great experience for me as well.

I soon went into the army and it was very difficult at first. I did BMT like everyone else and what kept me sane was listening to the sets of my recordings to remind myself that when I was finished with the army, that was what I would go back to and it helped me through a difficult time as a sort of softie musician serving in the army. For some reason they thought I was combat fit.

Now, after finishing my military training I was to go straight into the Music and Drama Company or so I thought, but back in the day before computerisation they lost my file and they said, "No, no record of you going to the Music and Drama Company" and off I went to the School of Military Medicine which was very difficult because I thought I would be back on the piano soon after BMT. Instead, I was carrying stretchers and full packs running up and down Peng Kang Hill.

Indeed it was a difficult time and they sent me to a unit as a medic after I passed out of, not passed out on a parade field, but after I passed out of the school of infantry training and I went to a unit, one of the SIR (Singapore Infantry Regiment) units, as a medic in the clinic or the medical centre and a few days later they found my file and said, "Oops, you're supposed to go to the Music and Drama Company" so I went there for a while and there was one instance of me working under the then Lieutenant Tony Wei who really taught me many things. I

remember that they asked me to do big band arrangements for large ensembles that I had never done before and every time that I didn't get it right they would send me to guard duty so I got really good at it very quickly. Leaving the army was wonderful, although I did enjoy my time there, and I went on, continued in my professional career, playing in bands and getting more and more serious about Jazz.

And in the late '80s I was very fortunate. In 1988 two very significant things happened to me — I got invited to play on the main stage of the Montreux Jazz Festival which really helped me to become a bit more recognisable in the world of Jazz and also in 1988 I helped to found the Composers and Authors Society of Singapore Limited which administers copyrights for composers and other music rights owners in Singapore. And the rest of it is pretty much mundane, boring career-related stuff. But people ask me what I do for a living and I say that what I do for a living is: I play the music I love, with the people I love, for the people who love me, so all of that went into my music. Thank you.

Forum

Arnold Gay: I've met a few celebrities, a few composers and musicians in my life, but I have to say, you're probably the least flamboyant musician, you know, considering your standing in the world of Jazz and what you've done and what you've achieved. How is that?

Jeremy Monteiro: I guess in the world of pop, being a celebrity or being famous is very integral to that of the life of a pop musician. But as a Jazz musician I think the celebrity is a by-product. My focus is really on making the best music I can and the press and the media, they are very kind. People listen to my music, they are very kind to speak well about me most of the time and so I don't want to be in this thing called "celebrity" and the persona. I guess I don't want to be the kind of persona created which I look at and I say "Okay, not too bad" but who is actually this guy who loves to play music and loves his friends and family.

Arnold: You didn't really grow up in a family of musicians, did you? Like your dad, he was a policeman, right? But he was a part-time musician as well. In fact, there were three of you, two of you actually went on to become professional musicians, your sister Claressa also works with me at Kiss92, you have another sister who went on elsewhere, how would you explain, I mean is it all down to the fact that your father was a part-time musician? Does it explain fully the path that you had growing up choosing to become a professional musician? By the time you were 15, that was your chosen path in life. Is there anything in particular that moulded you or made you decide that music was going to be your life choice?

Jeremy: Actually my dad was very serious. I think basically his job as a policeman and later as a motor oil executive was funding his life as a musician and really all he wanted to do at that time was to play music. And he had a wonderful record collection that he played all the time. Classical music and Jazz was always playing around the house so it was part of the environment for me growing up and of course after a while, I started buying my own records and looking for things on the radio. At that time on radio you could hear quite a lot of Jazz so I think music was always all around me and my mum actually practiced piano all the time. And in fact, when I was learning classical piano she wouldn't let me learn pop or Jazz but when she started learning pop piano and I would be in my bedroom, and would just open the door and look at her have her pop piano lesson and sort of had the lesson second-hand as well.

Arnold: You talked about your growing years, you talked about SJI, you talked about your parents. Did your parents ever tell you that they would prefer that you would have been something else, right at the beginning when they saw the first signs of you wanting to go into music? You know, "get real Jeremy, you're not going to make any money from this, be a policeman", or something like that?

Jeremy: Well my mum actually supported me all the way. I guess mothers do that, you know, they kind of just let you do what you want to do and encourage you. My dad was also very, very encouraging all the way until I said, "Hey dad, I think I want to become a professional musician," and then poof, he started discouraging me and he said he was going to stop paying for the lessons and basically he was very upset. He wanted me to do something more serious — become a doctor or lawyer or whatever the intention is. So yeah, it was like that. I guess for music and art and some other callings I'm sure, it really is a calling. You know deep inside this is what you want to do and no one can convince you otherwise if you really feel that that's your calling. Bitten by the arts or the music bug.

Arnold: So was there a time when you made that first jump into being a Jazz musician at 15 or 16, playing in that band of 35, 40-year-olds that "Oh my goodness, I've made the wrong decision.

Maybe I should have listened to my dad." What was it that kept you going?

Jeremy: You know I think that because by the time I was about 18, just before I went into army, my dad already saw that at a young age I could support myself, he stopped discouraging me. My dad went back to being very, very encouraging and all the way till his passing in 1993 he was very, very encouraging, you know, so all the way I had really good family support. He would come to my performances, he and my mum would come to my performances on a regular basis and at first I felt intimidated. I remembered the school concert at SJI in 1975 when I was performing and I said, "Mum and dad, can you please come and watch the show?" So they thought that I was going to be playing the piano but Hilarion had asked me to play the drums on the song "Let Me Be There" by Olivia Newton-John. So you know, they went, they sat down, I actually forgot to tell them I wasn't playing the piano and then you know the song goes and I could see their heads thinking about all those thousands of dollars of piano lessons wasted on drums.

Arnold: I have to ask you about SJI as well. Do you think it would have been any different if you were in any other school? I mean, how important was the

influence of St Joseph's in helping you decide, helping you, encouraging you in what you were trying to do, helping you forge that path?

Jeremy: I think besides the proximity to both City Music, the music shop to the school and Hilarion's house, you know that was big, that was huge, and so many of us, Hilarion, Ricky, became musicians. I was in the school military band as well, I played the clarinet. In the symphonic band I was playing the herald trumpet which plays all those very high notes that people normally pass out when they play. But I was aware and I had a big breath and I was able to play the high notes. But I think some people were very, very influential, I think besides my teacher, Mr Tan in Sabah, the next very important influence I had was former Brother Joseph Guan who was the bandmaster and teacher. He was just very influential to me because I believe he took something else for his Bachelor's degree but for his Master's he actually did music, French horn and acoustic guitar, Spanish guitar. And he was very encouraging. He would sit down and give me pep talks and so on, and I think that's probably who, besides Mr Tan, who really cemented my interest and focus and so if I didn't go to SJI that would have never happened, so I live a very serendipitous life, I always meet the right people at the right time. I will always be at the right time at the right place and I think that being at SJI at the right time and the right place and having the right talents are some of the many blessings I am very thankful for.

Arnold: Obviously you went conventionally up to 'O' levels, but you didn't really talk about how you actually honed your skills. How did you swim, did you seek any mentors? How important do you feel mentorship is in the industry?

Jeremy: I think in the world of arts whether you decide to go for your tertiary education or not, I think the

most important thing to learn is to learn how to teach yourself and to learn critical self-awareness. Learning to teach yourself — because once you learn how to teach yourself, you don't really need to be always around teachers and I think Bro Joseph Guan and Mr Tan Tze Tong were instrumental in teaching me how to teach myself, that's one.

The other thing is to have a true critical self-awareness. You know, very often people can't really gauge at what level they perform a particular task, duty or function accurately. It's almost like combing your hair without a mirror in front of you and I think that if you learn how you do, anything you do, be it a task or a job, whatever, with an accuracy just like you're combing your hair in front of a mirror with a true critical self-awareness then you find that you can propel yourself forward.

My teachers, other than my form teachers earlier, were records. I would really dissect the records (audio recordings) I listened to and this is very common in the world of Jazz musicians, who learn by listening and breaking apart and transcribing and capturing not just the notes but the essence and style and spirit of the particular performer and this is how I managed to learn to play.

And of course as I started my professional career I had the opportunity to

meet many great musicians while growing up, people like James Moody, one of the pillars of Bebop Jazz, Toots Thielemans who is still alive and well, playing music professionally. And many, many great performers to whom I would never be afraid to ask questions or people; sometimes when I got to be a little bit well known and I was playing in a small festival where I was the headlining act, if I heard a piano player who was just a backing player for a singer who knows something or used something that I didn't know, I would actually go up to them and say, "Can I take a lesson or two while we're here, how much do you charge?" And I would take the lesson in my hotel room.

And I think we must never stop doing that, actually going up to people who know something that we don't know and because of pride or "face", we should never be afraid to ask people to teach us.

Arnold: You have some fancy titles next to your name Jeremy, FRSA, FLCM…what exactly are they?

Jeremy: It's interesting because I was very honoured to receive the LASALLE College of The Arts professorship some years ago, in 2006, a few years after I got a call from the LASALLE president Professor Robert Ely I thought to myself "I'm a professor but I've just got 'O' levels so maybe I should go and get some other paper qualifications." So I wrote to the London College of Music and I said, "Can I get a dispensation of all the preceding grades and requirements, because I'm already a practicing professional and can I take the fellowship examination at the London College of Music, so that I could have a piece of paper which says I can do what I can do?"

Arnold: That's pretty impressive.

Jeremy: And then when I was at LASALLE, one of the other leaders over there introduced me to the fellowship of the Royal Society for the Encouragement of The Arts, Manufactures and Commerce (The RSA) in the UK and I was elected as a Fellow over there.

Arnold: So coming back to your career now, you've had 20 albums, you've supported, you've recorded with 200 artists, do you still enjoy it? I sense the passion when you speak but do you really, honestly still enjoy doing what you do? I know you spend a lot of your time, half the time of the year perhaps, travelling in the region, performing in the region, do you still feel the fire and the energy for Jazz?

Jeremy: Well actually I play for free, they pay me to travel but I hate airports. Getting to a place is very difficult. Yes, the short answer is that I can't imagine doing anything else than playing, composing and teaching music. It's really my life, you know? It's really so much. I think you can't really be an artist or musician at all if you didn't love it. I mean right now, the fact of the matter is that I am also involved in the music business and to me, I find that a necessity so that I can earn a decent living but quite honestly, if I had my choice, if I ever won a big lottery or won a big windfall, all I would want to do is lock myself up with a piano and play, and go out and play gigs whether they paid me or not.

Audience: Were there any doubts on your mind during your career in music and wondering if this was the right thing for you? Were there any difficult times or low points along the way?

Jeremy: Of course along the way I had my doubts and most of the time it's getting myself into trouble by, I'm not really a businessman person, as a businessman I've gotten myself into trouble a few times, I've opened and closed seven recording studios in the '80s. They say the definition of insanity is doing the same thing over and over again and expecting different results and I must be pretty insane to have done that. Seven recording studios and recently I actually went in with a friend to rescue studio number 8, Lion Studios, which is like Singapore's equivalent of the Abbey

Road studios, and they were sort of troubled and my friend David Tan and I went in to rescue it.

So here I am after number 7 swearing to never do it again, and getting involved in number 8. And of course, every time something like that happens it's a low point. I remember when my jingle company did very badly in the early '90s and I sold out to Rediffusion which was owned by the Arab-Malaysian Bank in Malaysia, and they asked me to move to Malaysia and after a while, because of the Gulf War, the economy was very bad they said they wanted to close down the Singapore office. I said, "I didn't sell you my baby in order to close down the

Singapore office. And if you are going to close the Singapore office then I am going to quit." And because I wasn't very smart, I had hired a very good number 2, they told me to go ahead and quit. And I came back to Singapore with very little money, with my family, with my tail between my legs and started all over again. So those were low points. But my low points have always been, you know, just mistakes and decisions I've made, my own fault.

Arnold: There was also a phase in your career where you went off and started composing National Day songs, I think you co-wrote or co-composed national songs, "One People, One Nation, One

Singapore" I suppose is the most famous? Was that a particular phase of your career? Was it something you had to do? Something you wanted to do?

Jeremy: I think I didn't really feel this way back then but I met a very great musician from Italy one time. He was working on some music and he's based in Bangkok, he actually writes scores for all the Thai horror movies and you know, I was working on some music with him in his home studio and he said, "Let me take a break" and he went downstairs then he started drawing on this blueprint for someone's kitchen cabinets and then after that he would say, "Let's walk over to my restaurant" and he took me to one of the restaurants near his house and he cooked a beautiful meal so I said, "How do you go from being a chef to an interior designer to a musician, you know?" He says, "Where I come from, in Milan, creative expression is creative expression, these are just modalities of it you use as an outlet." And he just went from one to another. And I guess I don't know how to cook nor can I design anyone's kitchens cabinets but I love to apply myself across different genres though I'm known as a Jazz musician. In 1991 when I wrote a classical-folk overture, creative and won a silver medal for Best Music Score at the International Radio Festival, New York, and it's not Jazz. And I've played on 300 pop records and when I was asked to work on campaign songs, government

campaign songs, I was the musical director for "Stand Up for Singapore", "Count On Me Singapore", "We Are Singapore" and I was the composer of "One People, One Nation, One Singapore".

Arnold: You weren't coerced, were you?

Jeremy: I wasn't coerced at all! And you know quite honestly working with Ernie Watts who is a great Jazz musician, he played thousands of pop records and I asked him, "How do you play this sort of really mundane pop tunes, you know some of them are not very nice, but you put in your heart and soul and tell yourself that the songs are really so wonderful" and he says that when he is in the studio and the music is put in front of him, he just looks at it as the most amazing piece of music ever written in the history of music and he believes it like that in the three hours that he's in the studio. So if I am working on something that is not really nice, and even if think that this is not really my normal expression, while I'm doing the job, and I think this can apply to any job right, you just tell yourself: this is the most important, amazing piece of music. And when you have that attitude you put your heart and soul into it, then of course when it's over you collect the money, you walk and never have to listen to it again, unless you like it.

Br. Armin
A. Luistro FSC

∾

Secretary
Department of Education
Republic of the Philippines

Born in Lipa City, Batangas, Br. Armin finished his elementary and secondary education at De La Salle Lipa. He earned his Bachelor of Arts degree in Philosophy and Letters at De La Salle University — Manila, where he also obtained his Master's Degree in Religious Education and Values Education. He completed his doctorate degree on Educational Management at the University of St La Salle in Bacolod City. He was conferred an Honorary Doctorate in Humane Letters (honoris causa) by La Salle University in Philadelphia, USA. A true-blue Lasallian, he has now pledged to see to the education concerns of every Filipino child.

Br. Armin has also served as board trustee, chairperson or director in various non-La Salle institutions such as the Catholic Education Association of the Philippines (CEAP), the Asian Institute of Management (AIM), the ASEAN University Network (AUN), Assumption College, the International Association of University Presidents (IAUP), the

Association of Southeast Asian Institutions of Higher Learning (ASAIHL), and the SIDHAY Foundation for street children. He has given countless speeches on education, university development, stewardship, responses to national crises, and networking.

I will just share a little story. Monday will be the first day of school for our 46,000 public elementary and secondary schools in the Philippines. So, between now and this weekend, this is a wonderful respite for me. In the past several months, we have been preparing each one of those 46,000 schools to better serve the Filipino learners. In preparation for this talk, I tried to contextualize the education system in Singapore, and I realised that there is a big difference between the number of schools in Singapore and the Philippines. When I think of a country of 5.3 million and remember that I have to face about 21 million students in the public schools on Monday, I realised that I'd love to be in Singapore a little longer.

My task in the country is to be able to ensure the effectiveness of the work of the 640,000 Filipino teachers. I was told that the number of teachers in Singapore is around 34,000. We just hired 61,000 this month to fill the gap in our teaching force this year.

One time I was addressing our teachers, I told them if we wanted to change our country, the only thing we need is to start a revolution. I reminded them that the Philippine police and the Philippine army totals around 340,000, while the work force in the Department of Education is around 670,000. We can easily outnumber the police, the Philippine army and all the men and women in uniform; we can start a revolution. I told them that the only real lasting revolution is one that involves the education of its people.

I am a reluctant leader. If one would imagine me in high school, one would never think of me as a leader, much more a cabinet member in the Aquino administration. I was a mediocre student; I would not raise my hand to answer during the class unless the teacher called me up. I am more of a follower than a leader. If I did anything epic, it was only because the real leader was out of the room and I felt myself to be the next best substitute to someone who was not there.

When I look back at my life, what I have gone through is essentially what I have seen in SJI and SJI International. There is nothing that separates me and the students whom I've talked to earlier with Brother George. They are talking about their dreams, and speaking about diversity and the wonderful things they are learning inside the Lasallian institution. What I do in the Department of Education is one that I've learnt. If you look at my CV, there is nothing but La Salle from elementary all the way to my doctorate degree. I thought that what I'm doing now is something that we're supposed to do anyway.

One of the wonderful things I do is visit our 46,000 schools, at least in my dreams. In the past 35 months, I have visited around 303 schools all over the 17 regions in the country unannounced. That's an average of around eight schools per month. And I was counting, if I did that religiously for 480 months, I should be half the age of Methuselah in the Bible, the oldest living man, to be able to visit every one of those schools.

Brother George asked me, "So, have you been surprised when you visited the schools?" I said, "No, I surprised them." I surprised the principals who were not in school when I came in. I surprised the teachers who were not teaching when I sat quietly at the back of the room. And after 10 minutes the teacher stood up, noticed me, looked at the photo, looked at my face, looked at the photo again, and said "Brother Armin? Is that you?" I must have caused a lot of consternation among our teachers for taking the time to actually visit our schools.

But the wonder of wonders is that for every school I have visited, the only thing I do, seriously, is to enter the classrooms and sit with the students at the back. You do not know what kind of anxiety and stress the teacher in front goes through when they see me sitting at the back of the room for these offbeat visits.

But I have a secret to share. I do not look at the teacher. When I sit at the back of the room, I actually look at the eyes of the students in that room. And when I see that they are engaged, then I know there is a teacher, a good one, a dedicated teacher in that school.

It only takes me around three minutes as I enter the gate of the school to know whether there is a dedicated principal, and whether there is a set of teachers who love their students. It's easy — you go inside the gate, you look around the garden, you check if there's trash or vandalism, you check whether the windows are broken, you go straight to the washroom and smell if it pleases you. If they fail the test, there is no one in the school who cares for the students.

I've always felt that what I do now, whether it is ensuring that we build 66,800 classrooms or hiring 61,500 teachers or putting up 90,000 toilets for our 46,000 schools, is not one that an educator should even be bothered with. But committed teachers know that our task is not purely just to teach. Our task is to make sure that the environment where our students go to is one where they will thrive and enjoy, where they will be safe, and where they will know that there's someone there who cares sincerely for them.

I do not know what plans God has for me, but the task that is before me today is one that is challenging, to say the least. Exciting even, if we want to look at the different learning environments one is placed in. When I left De La Salle Philippines, I was in charge of around 100,000 Lasallians in 18 schools. Little did I know that leaving La Salle was like jumping from the frying pan straight into the fire. And handling 20 million students in 46,000 schools is not a joke. If I can address you today, it is because I am not in my country, and I am not thinking of those 20 million students. This is a nice respite. I hope I can stay here a little longer.

Forum

Audience: Has anybody ever tried to bribe you, and what was your response?

Br. Armin Luistro: On my first day in office, a box arrived, from someone anonymous. When I asked my secretary to open it, there were around 12 bottles of expensive alcohol — hard liquor. I think it came from a supplier. I told my secretary, "Please return it to whoever left this box and tell them I don't drink." (I'm lying — I actually do, but I don't drink from bottles whose patrons I do not know.) That was my first time and that was my first day in office.

I was told that in the Philippine government, the estimated amount of leakage because of corruption is around 30 percent to maybe 40 percent of the actual budget. That does not include what suppliers will bring in and give to you, either in kind or actual cash.

In one conference where I was to meet all of the superintendents, I was at the lobby of a hotel and I noticed a lot of unfamiliar faces. I asked around and they said they're actually suppliers of textbooks. I went straight to a conference room, I gathered all of our superintendents, and I gave this rousing speech. I told them, "Do you know how much it takes for a department to be labelled as corrupt?" There was silence. I said,

"One. You only need one superintendent to be picked up from the airport by an SUV, brought to a nice hotel, and be treated to a nice and expensive dinner by a textbook supplier and be photographed. If that lands in the papers tomorrow morning, the whole department will be labelled as corrupt." At the end of that rousing speech, the unfamiliar faces disappeared from our conference room.

I told our Filipino businessmen in the Philippines, "What do you want?" They said, "Brother, only one thing. We want a level playing field." I said, "Okay, I'll do all of these things." I gave them a list of things to do. We'll go transparent, we'll publish everything in the web, and we'll have the civil society to serve our bidding process. But I told them, "But that's not enough. Don't you know that for every corrupt government official, there are ten of you trying to bribe us? If you want a level playing field, you better do your own part." I do not know if the image of the department has changed, but we deal with these types of individuals almost on a daily basis. You just have to be headstrong and be clear about it.

Arnold Gay: I want to read off some figures here. These are official figures, officially declared wealth figures of several Philippine Cabinet Ministers.

Filipino Foreign secretary: $21 million
Filipino Defense secretary: $8.1 million

Some Department of Education secretary called Brother Armin: net worth $16,400.

How do you fend off the temptations? Don't you sometimes feel "Hey, I could be doing a lot better"?

Br. Armin: My problem is I go back to the community and they learn I have $16,000 and they tell me "You're rich!" Yes, I'm the poorest cabinet member, but my secret is that I'm also the happiest,

and I mean that. I don't go around with security. And, with apologies to our beloved ambassador, I am not comfortable with protocol and people meeting me at the airport. I travel alone because I don't have money. If someone comes to me and says "Give me all the cash you have", I will give him everything I have. That won't make me poor. I reside in the Brothers' community at De La Salle University. I don't need to pay for my lodging. I have a community of Brothers who will feed me and pray with me. And the great thing is that there are a lot of freedoms one stands to gain because one doesn't have money. I can take the light-rail train and not have to look for parking. I can go to a nice conference and not have to pay for my dinner, because somebody richer than me will treat me. So, it's not too bad, it's not too bad.

Arnold: You describe yourself as a very average student, unwilling to lead. But still you did well, did your master's, became the university president, joined a long political campaign which left you out in the wilderness, and now you're a cabinet minister.

Br. Armin: True. If I were one of the students in SJI International now, I wouldn't think of myself as a prospective future leader. If there's anything I've accomplished, it is proof that ordinary people can do so much because you're

dedicated to that role and that ambition. I think part of leadership asks us not to have to know everything and to be able to do everything. Part of the tasks of a good leader is to be able to choose people who can join your team, whom you can trust and work with. I've been blessed with an excellent executive team. And none of my Undersecretaries and Assistant Secretaries are political. They all came from the private sector and they have invested a lot to do something at this stage in their lives.

Arnold: So you're saying you surround yourself with people who are smarter than you. Is that why you've succeeded where people before you have not been able to, in terms of meeting the needs of your country's education, and pushing through all these reforms like hiring 60,000 new teachers and establishing 76,000 new schools?

Br. Armin: The important contribution of the Aquino administration to the education reforms is twofold: first, we were able to address the most critical shortages of inputs in education. Second, we were able to push for — with political will — the most significant reform in the curriculum, and that's the K to 12 program.

When we came into office, I said that the first thing we need to do is to assess where we are, and to report to the nation our real shortages. We said that we needed five important inputs into Philippine education so that we will be able to address that. First we needed 100,000 teachers, we needed around 70,000 classrooms, we needed 90,000 toilets, we needed around six million textbooks and maybe around three million armchairs. We published this, and then we did three things.

First, we asked the new administration for a bigger-sized budget. In the past two budget seasons, the Department of Education has had the biggest increase in our share of budget. Second, we called a number of our stakeholders and told them, "Don't corrupt us and we will be transparent with you." I think that brought down the corruption to a manageable level, I will not say zero, but maybe less than 10 percent. And certainly because civil society and private groups and NGOs saw that we were serious about those five shortages which we published, they helped us. Third, we started the most controversial reform of the Philippine education system, adding two years. We did that by holding hundreds of consultations. I explained the program maybe a hundred times, listened to every single argument, not that I took notes of all of them, but they gave me a sense of where we were. My strategy was to listen to everyone, tire them out, let them come up with all possible objections, be clear with what we wanted them to accomplish, be humble, and accept that it will not be a perfect solution, and push on with what we could do today and not wait for tomorrow.

I'm happy to report that as of December last year, we were able to address all the shortages for textbooks and chairs. This year, we will be able to address the other three shortages. The President signed into law the Enhanced Basic Education Act of 2013 on May 15, feast of St John Baptist de la Salle.

Audience: You mentioned the basic education system, 12 years altogether. In your opinion, what is the impact that this particular law will have on the global competitiveness of the students after 12 years?

Br. Armin: Just three things. One, prior to the signing of this Philippine law, there are only three other countries in the whole world that continue to have less than 12 years of pre-university — those are the Philippines and two other countries in Africa. Number two, our enhanced basic education puts the Philippines at the same standard as the rest of Asia. As you know, in 2015 we will have the ASEAN integration, and it is important for the Philippines to be able to have the same qualifications framework as the other ASEAN countries; otherwise, we will never be competitive. Third, in order to let people attain those standards, it requires an actual review of our curriculum, so that Filipinos will know and be able to be competitive. Part of the basic problem of the Philippines is that the best private schools already have 12, if not 13, years of basic education. They have K1, K2, and grade 7. When our public schools' students compete with the private school graduates for university slots, they are really two years behind in exposure and whatever background they have. It is important for any educational system to be able to provide access to all in an equitable fashion. And I do not think public school students are unable to access university because they are not intelligent. It is because we do not provide them with the same opportunities as those who are in private schools. So, in my mind, we'll have to provide the same opportunities for all Filipinos. It is a way of equalising so that even those in public schools can compete with those in private schools.

Audience: K to 12 was also meant to reduce poverty incidence so students who finish Grade 12 can now work without pursuing a college degree. But a lot of Filipinos, especially those at the poverty level, are complaining that they will be burdened now with more expenses, because they now have to send their children to school for 12 years.

Br. Armin: We know that education provides access to many opportunities. But education is not a guarantee that you will move out of poverty. That's another question altogether. The task of the government and of all serious educators is to make sure that we provide that opportunity to all. With respect to better access to jobs and with respect to jobs, part of the reform is ensuring that middle-level skills will have their rightful place in the Philippine economy. Unlike the other developed economies, the Filipino obsession to get a college diploma has not really ended up in more Filipinos moving out of that cycle of poverty because it has just simply created more fly-by-night universities and colleges, of standards that are not of the same levels as the universities are meant to be.

Secondly, part of our difficulty is professionalising middle-level skills. People look down on vocational and technical skills. But a country that needs to develop would need not just carpenters but professional carpenters. We need to ensure that we have vocational and technical schools of quality, very much like what you have here in Singapore.

Prior to the development of the programme, we had a chance to look at the Singapore programme. One of the questions I asked the minister was "How are you able to transform your own vocational schools into one that is respected even by Singaporeans?" He said "Simple. We transformed the old schools and came up with facilities that looked much better than some of our university campuses. Instantly, the perception of students, teachers and general public was "This is not just a vocational school. This is a professional technical educational institution." I think that's what we need to do in the Philippines.

And how can you drive students who aren't proud of themselves? We need to come up with reforms that will transform the perceptions of the general public and the best way to do that is to make sure that we're able to communicate to the general public that there is dignity in work. And that one who has vocational skills, and maybe middle-level technical skills is as dignified as somebody who has a professional degree. It is not only about the capacity to earn, it's more than that. It is the capacity to gain self-respect and respect for one's job.

Arnold: Before you became the Secretary of Education, when you were president in the University, you waged a five-year campaign against the previous administration at some consequence to your own personal well-being and potentially your own career as well. Can you tell us why you did that and why you felt that it was so important?

Br. Armin: Prior to my appointment in the cabinet, I was president at De La Salle University. We were about to celebrate our centenary. All of my projects, programmes, were in anticipation of the 100th year of De La Salle University. But sometime in 2005, there was political turmoil in the country because of the national elections in 2004. Essentially, the allegation was that there was a lot of cheating and pressure on the part of our election officials to ensure the victory of the (then) incumbent president. As University President, I was also concurrently teaching a class when news came out that the President apologised and acknowledged that she called an Election Commissioner; that did not sit too well with me. I was connecting that with what I was teaching in class. I felt I had no credibility or moral authority to tell my students in class "Don't cheat" unless I had the same courage and moral conviction to say publicly, "I cannot accept the President saying, 'I cheated or at least pressured the Commissioner of Elections to cheat on my behalf.'" I was very divided and I felt I needed to speak out against that.

To cut the story short, several candidates in a forum talked about it and the De La Salle Brothers came into the picture. We brought that discussion with other Religious and many of them said, "Yes, our convictions tell us that we must ensure that we speak against corruption, we speak against dishonesty, and therefore, we have to say our piece." When the De La Salle Brothers published our statement, the other Religious hid in their convents. The way it ended was we found ourselves standing alone, speaking truth without those who we thought were with us from the start.

Arnold: Did you expect it to take as long as it did?

Br. Armin: No. I prayed hard and I complained to God. From 2005 till July 2010, it did not seem our efforts would bear fruit. It was a five-year battle. It challenged everything we know. It was a question raised against the very soul of the nation. And the depression I went through was one that made me reach the point where I asked, "Is this worth the fight because no one seems to be listening?" I felt very bad, the other Brothers felt very bad. But I did not feel I could continue to be a teacher in the classroom advocating honesty and truth to our students if I also did not do the same when I looked at what was happening in our nation. Worse, I felt I was cheating my students, preparing them for the world beyond, and telling them, "You have to be honest, you have to be moral," and not doing something about a Philippine society that was decaying and losing its moral ground. I felt I had to be truthful, and if that was a lost cause, I would rather continue this advocacy even if it did not bring success as I expected.

Arnold: Did you feel that you were in danger at any time during the five years?

Br. Armin: I did, but I kind of swept that under the rug. Advocacies in the Philippines usually come with published statements and signatures. It also involves bringing warm bodies to the streets. We do that with our robes, with linked arms marching in the cities.

Arnold: But how did they threaten you? Did you get knocks on the door in the middle of the night, did they cut off your water, or take away your car?

Br. Armin: They scare you off by actually gathering supporters, by bribing journalists to write against you, the

people you love and the school you come from. During that five-year period, we called the journalists "envelop-mental" journalists because they get their regular envelopes at the end of the month, and they will write against you and everything bad about La Salle or maybe about me. There was one journalist who would write about my sporting a moustache. I don't know how that is connected, but that was the first time in my life that even my moustache was a matter of national consequence.

But that's not that bad. The worst part of the experience is people whom you work with in the university, your own alumni dropping you like a hot potato. The worst of that was when one of our alumni supporting our basketball team decided in the middle of the season "Sorry, the rest of the funds are not coming." And so we had nothing for our basketball players, our staff, nothing at all. Every experience you go through makes one ask the question: "Is this worth fighting for?" And I suppose every leader, and every person of conviction, will go through that testing period. At least, I hope so.

Arnold: In hindsight, would you have done anything differently?

Br. Armin: I considered that in different instances. But my response to that every time would be I would not be able to face myself the next morning in the mirror and have respect for myself. I figured I could lose the respect of anyone else, even the ones I love, but if I stand in front of the mirror and lose my self-respect, then everything is lost. And if that was the only thing that kept me in the fight, then maybe that was it.

Audience: A famous quote by Nelson Mandela: Lead from the back and let others believe they are in front. People have many interpretations of that. Does it mean anything or apply to you?

Br. Armin: Let me answer it this way. I told you from the beginning, I am a reluctant leader. If there's anyone in the room who is willing to lead, I will be your second. I obviously see myself as the one who'd support the leader in front. I'm not naturally articulate, if I'm articulate now, it's because I had to go to each school and they would ask me to give a little speech. I learned the hard way. I'm happier in the background.

The moments in my life when I saw myself taking on leadership positions was because the one in front had either given up or absconded and ran away from the fight. I'm not the kind of person who would leave if the project is not finished. I believe leaders choose to put themselves in a box that reads: "first in, last out". I'm happy to wash the dishes after everyone has left the party. Sincerely, I'm that type of a leader. And in these different situations in my life, including the advocacy for truth, it was only because there was no one else, and someone said, "You'll be the spokesperson" and I said, "I'll do it only until the next willing leader comes in." That took a long time.

Arnold: Is that possible as Education Secretary? You have to fight political battles every day. How do you manage that? What happened to all the journalists who wrote bad things about

you? What do you do to people who make life miserable for you?

Br. Armin: I told you, one of the most wonderful strategies, at least in my experience of a good leader, is just to wear everyone out. Be the first one in, and be the last one out. And don't leave until you have accomplished your task. Most of the others will leave because they have something else to do; they have other interests, they're not serious about it, or they just have no more energy. Sometimes leadership requires that you stay there the longest.

Arnold: You still have to win over those who stay in the race. So there has to be some skill involved when you decide you're going to push a button and do something. How do you decide now is the time?

Br. Armin: Be a Brother. That is where you learn all the politics inside the community. But seriously, every week, or every two weeks, the Brothers in the community gather together and we discuss issues. Matters of life and death and trivial issues and we fight, and we debate, then after that, we pray and eat. That kind of experience moulded in me the sense of comfort in listening to the worst debates and disagreements without being disagreeable, and recognising that you don't have to fight with people.

We may come from different perspectives, we may not always agree, we don't have to be disagreeable. You can fight with me; I will not expand energy fighting with you. I have many other things to work on.

I was driving one Sunday, and one congressman called me up on my cellphone and he shouted at me. No one has ever shouted at me in my entire life as an educator. If you go into the public service, you eat humble pie. Public service is a thankless job. I have heard all types of criticisms about the K to 12 reform. If there were any supporters, they will come in trickles, and they come few and far between. For the K to 12 reform, I met with everyone; I heard every single argument against it. That gave me a feel of what the worst critics thought about our education reform.

But I was very clear about what we need to accomplish and why it was important. I was counting the number of years the current president, Aquino, who is supportive of the reform, had been in office. He has three more years. If we do that towards the latter part of his term, that would be an impossibility. It was important that we do that in the first half of his term. We felt that for some type of reforms, it is important that you do

Secretary of the Department of Education of the Philippines

THE FULLERTON - SJI LEADERSHIP LECTURES 0

presents

Br. Armin A. Luistro FSC
Secretary of the Department of Education of the Philippines

it at a time when you are able to gather support. You will never get 100 percent support, but you need the political will.

Audience: Br. Armin, you remind me of Pope Francis, doing away with all formalities. Does being a Brother make you freer to do what you really believe in? Some of the things you do, I'm sure if an ordinary secular minister did, would get a different reaction.

Br. Armin: At least in Philippine culture, that may be significant. But I think we are able to transcend the religious part. People are willing to give the benefit of the doubt to someone they sense as being sincere and does not have a political agenda.

Arnold: You taught in the university. Did that prepare you to be the Education Secretary? You took at least six weeks to decide before you said yes to Aquino.

Br. Armin: When the President asked whether I'd be happy to serve, I said "Mr President, I have five other nominees. They are more intelligent, they are better experienced, and they have a better track record than myself." He says, "But I don't know them and it's a position of trust." I told the president, "Well Mr President, it's not my decision;

I have to go back to my Brothers." I went back to my Brothers and some of my friends, and every single one whom I loved and respected, and whom I thought loved and respected me, said "No. Don't take the job." Seriously, this was one moment in my life where I did not have a single supporter. For the right reasons.

But let me go back to why I took on the challenge. I was about to sleep that night after six weeks of struggling. Everyone said "don't take the challenge." I slept that night but woke up in the middle of it with the thought, "If I wake up the next morning, face myself in the mirror, would I respect myself for that

decision?" That was how it hit me. For five years, we advocated truth, integrity, and reform in the Philippine government. For five years we spoke about how important it was to do all of these changes. All the La Salle schools and all the Lasallians were praying this prayer: "Let me be the change I want to see." I asked myself, "how can I face myself in the mirror and say, "We talked about it, we prayed about it, we asked for change, now I'm asked to do the change," and I say, "No — my journey, Mr President, ends here. I cannot continue on that path."

Maybe it was a wrong decision. But I told myself I would rather make a

mistake and still have that respect for myself, than not to engage. And then that's where I am now.

Audience: Teachers hold the greatest influence over the youth of today. I'd like to understand, from your perspective as the Secretary of Education, how you plan to guide teachers to be an inspiration to their students?

Br. Armin: I don't think any kind of reform will matter unless it begins in the heart of every teacher. But to be practical about it, we're faced with this dilemma. At least in the Philippines, we have more than 600,000 public school teachers. Not all of them have the heart to be a teacher. But they are already permanently hired. We could begin recruiting new teachers and include additional qualifications.

At the end of the day, we are left with human beings. Some of whom are fully dedicated. Others fall behind. It's like a normal bell curve. Whether you're a principal in a small school or handling 600,000 teachers in a national education system, you will always have this bell curve. The task of the leader and all the executives is to be able to develop programmes so that the ones who are dedicated teachers are able to influence those who are average, the bigger majority of teachers, and to create that environment where those who are rewarded are those who show dedication. The rest who are lagging behind, I don't know if you want to flush them out of the system. If it's legal to do so, then maybe you can.

But the reality is they will stay with you. In any major movement or change in the world, you don't need 100 percent dedicated people. You only need a core group who would be able to influence all the rest. Stick it out with this small group. You don't need a very big number. The scriptures on Christ say you only need 12 people to transform the world. One of them will be a Judas.

Arnold: Right now, you're working on the infrastructure; you're working on the numbers. What do you see down the road for the education system?

Br. Armin: For the next two, three years, I think the real revolution in Philippine education is really IT in education. It's not so much starting new computer laboratories per se, it's actually reforming the curriculum itself. So that it becomes attuned to the latest technology. I'm not fully sold on the idea of giving every child a laptop. I think you have to seriously study at what level technology is appropriate, because there are so many competencies that you cannot learn from technology.

Our challenge in Asia — Singapore, I'd like to include — is in the area of how exactly we use technology so that we make quality education accessible to all. The operative term for me is "to all". Not just developed countries in Asia, not just Singaporeans, or only those in private schools. Technology today allows us to develop software; some of them are already out on the net, that's open

source. That can actually be a solution to a lot of the big digital divide in Asia. I am an advocate of "copyleft" rather than copyright. I think there are some basics in education whether they are stories or modules that must be developed and not sold, and not be used exclusively by a few. I think it's our responsibility to make sure that every child, at least in this part of the globe, Asia, is educated well.

The only way we can do that is via technology. But I have to warn you, that the drivers of technology are businessmen, traders — they're not educators. And if you look at technology today, with what is the latest, most of it is really with the end in view of making money. My dream, at least in Asia, is to be able to get the educators to be the driving force behind what and where technology should be moving, because educators cannot just educate those in their classrooms. We know that once I educate one child, I have to ensure that this same module, this same lesson, is accessible to others. My prediction is that Asia's make or break — at least in the area of education — is how Asia and teachers, and educators will be able to use technology to make education accessible.

If this is successful, we will be able to educate every Asian, every young person

in this part of the globe. If we're not, the digital divide will be so wide, there will be a few winners and many losers. I fear for Asia if that happens, because that will not be a wonderful place to be in at the time.

KF Seetoh

∽

Founder of Makansutra,
Curator of the World Street Food Congress

Seetoh Kok Fye, better known as KF Seetoh (Class of 1978) was recognised as Singapore's Food Ambassador by then Singapore President Mr S.R. Nathan. The New York Times calls him a "food guide maven", while CNN hails him a "Guru of Grub".

After a decade of professional stints in the media industry, KF Seetoh put a lucrative photography business aside and started Makansutra, a company that celebrates street food cultures.

A champion for street food since 1997, Seetoh has written numerous regional street food guides, and oversees the editorial content for Yahoo! Singapore, Esquire, The New Paper, Huffington Post and a host of community publications. He has also produced and hosted eight food TV series, including Makansutra Raw which was aired on regional and local TV, and The Food Surprise on Discovery TLC Asia, and made several appearances in food and lifestyle TV shows worldwide, including The Vision, China's most-watched food and travel show with 400 million viewers, Anthony Bourdain's various programmes, and The Martha Stewart Show. He was also a guest judge in the Top Chef finale in its

Singapore instalment. He also operates one of Singapore's yummiest hotspots — Makansutra Gluttons Bay, a night-time food court offering some of Singapore's favourite street food.

In May 2013, Seetoh saw the inaugural launch of his brainchild — The World Street Food Congress, a 10-day celebration of street delights where 80,000 food lovers came together under one roof to enjoy a massive feasting jamboree with culinary delights from all over the world.

Forum

Arnold Gay: There is very little known about KF Seetoh as a boy, the Singaporean boy who grew up in some neighbourhood and enjoyed his food. Tell us about your growing years.

KF Seetoh: I was born in KK Hospital and grew up in a house along Geylang Lorong 3, and I was a Geylang boy for a while, first generation Singaporean. My father came from Guangzhou, China. I spent Primary 1 in Geylang English School, opposite Lorong 20, then Saint Michael's. Anyone remember Geylang English School? It was between Lorong 23 and 21. Gangsters everywhere. If my father didn't go to St Michael's School and bribe the principal, Mr Ho (laughter), I probably would have remained there and become some top gangster. Talent sees success everywhere.

Arnold: Geylang is famous for two things. We won't mention the first one, but the second is…?

Seetoh: Geylang is also an inspiration! On the evil side of Geylang, that is Kamasutra. On the other side is Makansutra. Whenever I walk past it (Geylang), I am immediately reminded of the two greatest sins.

Arnold: Kamasutra obviously played its part, but let me ask you about Makansutra. How important was growing up in food central (Geylang), in making you a food guru? Did you go around seeing food and sampling food from the hawkers around you?

Seetoh: I did Makansutra because I'm odd. I had a nice gig, professionally, in the Straits Times. That's Straits Times, not SPH, but that's another story. After about seven or eight years, I said, enough. I wanted to hack it as a professional photographer and I did pretty well. I was just living it up. Maybe when I was in my 30s, I said to myself, "You are in professional photography, where it's all about young blood and you are old at 34." And I realised I had to make the switch. So I took pictures, wrote and thought: I really love food, and there was nothing about Singapore's food culture.

This was unlike how Japanese food is celebrated, Thai food, but Singapore food? Not really. People loved it, but back in those days, it was seen as hawker food. Hawking in Singapore was seen as a profession…murderers, rapists and all that. So I said, okay, let's start a food guide. I got the money to start up Makansutra in 1996–1997 after suing a telco for violating my photography copyrights. When I started the food guide, it was tough. I remembered I launched it on day one at the Singapore Food Festival at Boon Tat Street. They closed the whole street for stalls which sold food, books et cetera. There was a guy down there — me — sitting on a crab cushion, holding up a giant fork and spoon like the logo. We just started

THE FULLERTON - SJI LEADERSHIP LECTURES II

presenting

Mr. KF Seetoh

Founder of Makansutra and Curator of the World Street Food Congress

Media Partner STRAITS TIMES

selling the book, it was so tough! So I told myself, "Let's try to sell a hundred books today." I came across this auntie, I said, "Auntie, do you want to buy my book?" She took a look and asked, "Is this the best char kway teow?" Then again I sat down and thought, she may not need the book but I need her. I need her to tell me, I needed people like her to tell me (about the best food). That was what started my journey of finding people like this, to energise your idea. So the book became a hit and the next thing that came was the website. We started this website in 1998 or 1999, then the TV shows. We did food courts. We did blah, blah, blah. But this whole journey was a journey of discovery. It is still a big green field for me to be selling food culture. Then people say, "Why are you selling food culture?" Even the Ah Lian knows what it is. But I say, food culture is this: the hawker sells the food, you eat the char kway teow, and you go "Wah!". He will sell the food, but the "Wah!" I sell. I try to encapsulate the "Wah!" into a business model. Very smoky right? (laughter) That's my business. How terrible is that?

Arnold: Did living and growing up in Geylang have anything to do with the idea?

Seetoh: It wasn't really the living in Geylang. I am an observer. You can't talk about life and business if you don't observe. You can't just sit down with your

laptop and go onto Google and write reports. You walk the streets and you look at people and take a look at their faces. Stand there and observe them with a kopi o at Lorong 18. You see how life is at that level, and people are at that level. You can hear their heartbeat and you get a lot of ideas. You grow up with that heartbeat there. That's where you get a lot of ideas.

Arnold: What was it like in SJI for you?

Seetoh: I'll tell you why I'm so proud of being in a boys' school. This is my story. When I was in photography, I did a lot of fashion shows. You were young, you were hip, you wear a bandana … All these fashion stylists will send their photos to

you and then there was this model I was shooting, she was sizzling… and single. At the end of the shoot, she came and said: "Hey Seetoh, don't you remember me?" I was thinking, you don't have to drop a pickup line on me, it should be the other way round. She goes on, "Do you remember SJI, Sec 3, Tech 2?"

I said, "Oh no, you are not Christine, you are Christopher, right?" I said, "Well done, you look beautiful. Where did you get that from, man! Pain or not? Pain or not?" (laughter) So we have those people, we have ministers, we have Father John Bosco who played football with me. We have everything. In school, the teachers told us to be the best of who you are. If you want to

be a hawker, the SJI hawker will be the best... Minister? The SJI minister will be the best. (laughter)

Arnold: Brother Godfrey and Brother Cowen were influential people in your life, particularly in an incident involving a taxi driver?

Seetoh: In school, I was a bit of a rascal. Not the top rascal but probably about 3rd or 4th, isn't that good? But we were very good in our sports, we were very active. We played football, we ran and swam, played badminton, played hockey. And they are not apps, these were real games. And you know in class, we had good friends but I don't know what kind of relationship we had, not poor, we were good friends but we would fight. There was this guy, Lam, I forget his full name. I still bump into him. For no reason, we would fight. We fought during lunch, just fight, okay lah! In those days the best place was that corner at the back lane, behind the barber, at Bras Basah Institute. It was the field, behind the back gate. Of course you must have a watch; someone has to keep watch at the door. And the next thing you know, news would spread. In those days there was no social media but everybody knew. Then Brother Godfrey came to know about it, and he said: "You want to fight is it? If you want to fight, do it properly. Make sure it's fair,

okay? Make sure everybody knows, otherwise, we won't know who won or lost. Just fight at the football field so that everybody can see. But do it after 6:20 when I am off duty." At 6:30, we met up, two of us down there at the field with about 50 supporters. Then fight! No knives, nothing. We took off our watch and everything. Boom, punch, kick. Okay, your turn. Then Brother Godfrey said, "How long do you think this will carry on? When do you all want to stop? Have you all solved anything yet?" We looked at him and said, "We don't know. You asked us to fight, so we fight." Next day, we became very good friends. Mr Lam is now a taxi driver. And I call him for a taxi. That's SJI.

Arnold: You have called food Singapore's sole saving grace. Do you still believe that?

Seetoh: I see food as a culture. It is the most democratic culture. When a hawker's food is no good, you vote. I was just having lunch at the hawker centre today, and I said, "If you feel the heartbeat of a food centre or hawker centre, that's where the Singapore soul resides". When you walk into a hawker centre, be it a CEO, or a colonel or a captain, they take off their badges and they are all equal. They come together with food. It is one of those biological acts people do together, through food.

A lot of people initially saw food as just a function. I want to eat chicken rice. I want to eat this. Now, people are now beginning to understand that it's a bigger part of our culture, especially maybe over the last, maybe, ten years when Singapore was beginning to lose a little bit of its identity. So to me, I can say that food saved my life because I understand more about you, my country, me through food.

As I was saying earlier, when I was a photographer in the '90s, I was covering weddings. Good money. I would dread it when it was a Teochew couple. It meant that you would have to wake up at 4am because of the Teochew bride. Any Teochews here? Are you married? Did you marry in the era when the wife had to leave before sunset? Or did you get married at Sentosa beach with a foam party-type wedding? Usually, before the bride heads off to the groom's house, she has to say a last farewell to the parents as a single woman. That has to be done before sunrise. It's like five-something in the morning. So Teochew weddings "pai tan" (hard to earn money). And then you went to the groom's house, did all the things, see all the food spread.

Over the years, you shoot all the Hokkien, Cantonese, Teochew, Malay, Indian weddings. You'll notice that the food is all different. Chinese is not Chinese. There're so many. That's why I understand food. I understand why; why the Hokkien people always drink "Too Thor" (pepper pig stomach soup). Any Hokkiens here? You know what I mean? And the Teochews always got "Orh Ni" (yam paste). You realise when you go back to their country. Then you'll see the Silk Road of food and Silk Road of culture and influence in Singapore. You know, over the years it has evolved. It's changing. I guess it's changing very, very rapidly. People are forgetting a little bit of this interesting colour and foods that gave our culture this sparkle, this character.

Arnold: We already have some really big names here, Michelin-starred chefs

and restaurants. Is this a good thing for the local food scene?

Seetoh: You know why the Michelin stars like Gordon Ramsay want to come? Because they want to go to the hawker centres. Seriously, I mean our government, they bring all this in, it's good; it lends character, international class, et cetera. But to be a true connoisseur and practitioner, one must go down to the soul of the streets to find the heart of the flavours here. So your top chefs like Bourdain, Ramsay, they go to the back lanes of Geylang and they meet JB Ah Meng and be dazzled by his salted egg crab, salted prawns or white pepper crab. They are floored by it, they get ideas. Is it doing anything? Yes, it does help promote the Singapore Inc.

character to the rest of the world. This is what I mean by exchanging but it also has its side effects.

Arnold: What side effects?

Seetoh: The side effects are that a lot of people are taken in by all this. They look overseas for this stardom in the world of culinary craft. They want to go to all these fancy culinary schools and become a Gordon Ramsay, when the thing they are naturally good at is right under their noses, your own food culture. So people are looking across, when people across are looking at our food culture. I have seen it many times. When the government announced that they were going to build ten more hawker centres in the Sengkang, Punggol

area, the first thing I said was, "Where on earth are your hawkers coming from?" Foreign talents opening hawker stalls? I mean, you go to the hawker centre to eat Adobo and Ma La? Ma La char kway teow, Ma La chicken rice and Adobo char kway teow? So the next thing is, yah, we will form a hawker committee. The Minister said they will form a hawker committee. All talk only. The next thing you know a bunch of university kids are starting a "Hawkerprise". Whatever that word means. They say, "Mr Seetoh, could you come and support us? We are encouraging our cohorts in the university to look into this field, to be part of it and enter the field, ex-graduates are becoming hawkers and taking over their fathers' businesses." So I said, "Sure, it's up my alley." I went and gave talks and speeches and then, later I looked at the kids and asked, "Is this a movement you came up with or is this a school project?" You guessed it. So I said, "So when you graduate, how?" "Maybe somebody else will take over lah," they replied.

So why should I support you? It's all talk again. All class projects. Culture cannot be a class project, especially food culture. Our food history must not be reduced to an app or a book.

Arnold: So how do we take this forward, and ensure it's not just a class project?

Seetoh: You need to transfer the talk into action. I think we need heroes. The younger generation need to see their young hero hawker who is up there appearing in shows, who's teaching, who's, you know, getting the queues and getting Facebooked every day, getting gigs to perform and demonstrate. Wah, steady lah. Hawker, hawker heroes, street food professionals, street food heroes. A lot of people know, they make money, you know. Some of these condos are bought by them, just waiting to sell it back to you at a profit.

But I guess the sexiness of being a hawker, the appeal is not there. It was because the last group of hawkers who really saw it as a necessary business, because they had to live, they had to eat, was in the late '80s. After that you do not see them coming into the line anymore. So the young assistant hawkers of the '80s are already in their 50s or 60s already. So that dark period of food culture lasted from the '90s all the way to 2000s. Nothing. Everybody was encouraged to be a doctor, lawyer and whatever, you know.

Now that we are addressing the cancer of this food culture, we have to address how we could clean up that little dark era, when people felt disdain for food culture. Very strange, they like it but not the culture. They like the food but not the culture. So what we need to do is, I guess, we have to create programmes and create heroes and stars, you have to create doors for people to walk into the industry and say, "Wow, this is a respectable industry." I was just telling Vincent (Anandraj) just now. Hawkers, I know them all... I know all their failures and successes. They tell me, "You know what, when I finish my work, I do the morning shift — early morning, late morning, lunch, brunch — and I finish at 6 o'clock, 4 o'clock, and I don't bring my work home even if I wanted to." Unlike many of you here today.

You bring your work back to the MRT, dinner and bedtime and you regurgitate it the next morning when you brush your teeth. All your work pressures are still there but hawkers, no!

Arnold: You're the only person I know who says that hawking is not as difficult as it seems or appears.

Seetoh: You stand there (and observe). I have seen hawkers who sit on a stool and fry, and every time they look up, people are there desperately waiting for their food. To a hawker, every head is $3 to $4. When he looks up and he sees 10 heads, it's $30. If he does that 10 times a day, it is $300 to $400 a day, $12,000 a month. Not bad, huh? Then you write off 30 percent for your cost of food. It is very lucrative. I suspect the richest hawker in Singapore is the nasi lemak stall in Boon Lay. I calculated, I know the guy very well. I went to sit six hours at his shop and see what on earth his success model is. That guys doesn't even open for dinner; he only opens after dinner. 9pm and closes at 5am. His nasi lemak has 16 ridiculous items, beyond your classic items. He caters to kids: sausages, hash browns… All the things that shorten your life. When you come, the queue goes all the way out to the car park. Okay, so that's his model: freshness, variety. His rice steamer is the army type, even hotels don't have them,

that cooks for hundreds of people. At any one time, the queue is 50 to 100 people long. Even when it rains, people would carry their umbrellas in the car park, and even at the corner of the hawker centre, it goes up. The Boon Lay hawker centre, Power nasi lemak. Do you all know? His sambal comes in a pot slightly the size of this podium. I am not kidding! The real success model is that he has got two guys in front, these are the things that Harvard should be studying… and these two fellows they take alternate customers. So each person handles three at a go, so if you are sixth in the line, you are already being served. And the guys knows if you are regular; by the time you reach the front, what you want is already on your plate, they just ask you want anything else. So they just up-sell a little bit. "Fresh, just came out," even if it's not. Just lie. They do as much as a few thousand portions a day, each averaging $3.50. He has up to 8 people working there and you can discount 30% for food costs and like nothing for rentals plus a few thousand bucks for utilities. Go do the math, he takes a fat cheque home each month. He doesn't even show up! Sick, right? He even pays his taxes too. He has big accountants to do his taxes.

Arnold: You were talking about how the big guys, Gordon Ramsay, you were talking about local hawker

THE FULLERTON - SJI LEADERSHIP LECTURES II

presenting

Mr. KF Seetoh

Founder, Makansutra and Creator of the World Street Food Congress

heroes, inculcating this kind of spirit... So I guess Gordon Ramsay having the competition against the local hawkers was a good thing?

Seetoh: The whole idea of bringing Gordon Ramsay was an idea of one of the head honchos at SingTel, not the bloggers, because SingTel wanted the bloggers to go and spread the word. I was asked to host that show and I met Gordon. So I was wondering what this was all about. Was SingTel trying to promote their own site, HungryGoWhere? No, you don't see their branding there at all, it's not up their alley. Food culture is not up HungryGoWhere's alley, it's about food

recommendations, where to eat, and bookings. So I was talking to Allen Lew, the number 2 guy there, who started this. I said, "What do you want to do this for?"

It took him very long and then he came out with something, "Oh, to promote food culture." That's a bit dreamy right? So, I think he just wanted to start something and see what happens, and he started a fire. I told him at the event, "Allen, you started a fire. How are you going to keep this going? Otherwise people will accuse you of all kinds of malicious intent behind what you do." So yes, opportunity wise, I hope to propose something to them to make

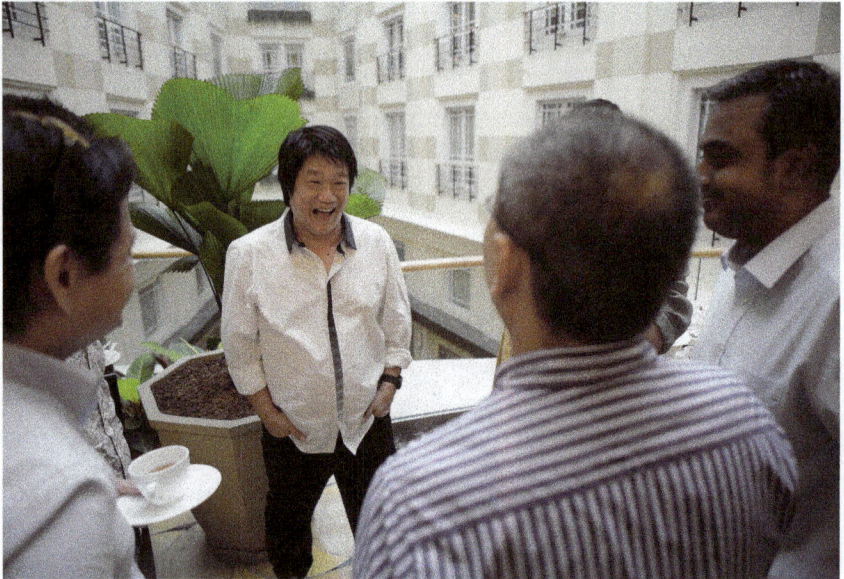

sure Makansutra is viable. When I spoke to Gordon, I had a private moment with him, I said, "Gordon, you're quite clever, you come to Asia, you cook Tom Yam there, I think you want to be known as the Asian Street Food Ang Mo Champion right? So you can go back to London and open an Asian Restaurant and say, "Look, I have the best chilli crab recipe. I beat the number 1 guy in Singapore." That's his model. What other interest would he have to come here? By the way, it was not Gordon Ramsay's recipe. It was Neo Catering's recipe.

Arnold: That's quite depressing. What about Anthony Bourdain? Someone you are a lot closer to. He really goes around trying all the local stuff… He appears to really believe in local food culture.

Seetoh: We exchange private emails. When he divorced his wife, I was the first to know and hear all the explicit details. He said, "The minute I made some decent money, my ex-wife filed for a split. She took what was legal and rode off into the sunset…" When his agent first called me, he told me that "Anthony Bordain appeared on Oprah and wrote his first book called Kitchen Confidential. He is coming to Singapore to do a show and if we were to do a show in Singapore, it would not be credible if you were not in the show."

Basically they were looking for a free guy to appear in the show. He was pretty nice. I was trying to get this agent to sell our books too. So I said yes. After I said yes, I was like, "Who the hell is this Anthony Bourdain?" So we set a time at 6:30pm that day and they asked, "Where shall we go?" I said, "I did not know". They loved that attitude. I said, "Call me at 5:30pm and I will let you know." So they called me and I said to meet at Sin Huat at Lorong 35, at Geylang. That famous crab noodle place. One plate of crab bee hoon costs $80 to $90. Their money what, I don't care. So we went there and I didn't know who Bourdain was, I didn't care, I just felt like eating and felt like splurging on a seafood meal. It is the most expensive seafood restaurant and it is in a coffee shop. Some of you might have been there. He was early. He was like a kid in Toys "R" Us. He went to see the live bull frog, touching the glass, watching the stingray, touching the crab. So *sua ku* (not well informed)! I said, "Hi, hello." And after all that, we got along and he said, "I love this food! What you said, food on TV and in books is like an oxymoron. You got to put it in your mouth, devour it, feel it, eat it, sin it."

We got down to talk, two of us ate about $700 worth of food. Paid by the agent, because it's their money. If you eat at

Lorong 35, Danny always brings out his signature dish: the crab bee hoon. Any of you tried it before? You know what I am talking about. He always brings it out last, you notice? No matter what you order, because after that dish, everything will be downhill. If he serves that dish first, everything will be downhill, so he always serves it last. So Anthony was eating all the scallops, prawns, sotong, everything and he loved it. When the crab bee hoon came, he smoked, had a beer and took a mouthful. He turned to the camera and started his monologue, "I've been served … VIP treatment…" on and on and on, eating and eating. He said, "After this meal, I would not mind if the world ended now." He turned to me and asked me what I thought. I said, "Why you all talk so much when there is food on the table? My mother always says, 'When there is food on the table, eat first, you never know where the next meal is coming from.' So we are very different. I see food, I eat, you see food, you talk."

He quoted me in his book. Nasty bits. See food eat lah, no food then talk. But I have seen him change over the years. He is quite an institution. He is not free to be himself anymore. He has a very fragile, very famous existence. He came to Singapore for the World Street Food Congress. You can see that he is a bit of a changed man. But he has to maintain

this very fragile, very powerful image of his.

Arnold: You've talked about food nostalgia before, and you associate it not just with the taste itself. You are talking about evoking memories, evoking emotions, you know. Do you think this is a critical component that is actually missing in today's food scene?

Seetoh: I saw a posting, I put on my Facebook today a picture of steamed minced pork with cartilage and some fat and some salted fish on top. It is a Cantonese classic. And I said something about, you know, when you have a terrible day, when you go back, you want to be reminded about the simple things in life and you want to reach out to comfort food. What is comfort food? And to me it was that. You take the meat and put it on some rice, and you do what the Cantonese say, you "pah fan", you claw the food into your mouth with the chopstick. People will sit cross-legged, I'm too fat, I can't cross my legs properly, and they will hold the bowl, and they claw the food. It is a very iconic, classic and comforting feeling and sight for me. It might remind you of the basics, where you came from, and food must mean that to you. So, if you are growing up, just be very aware of what works for you. It's rare, totally meaningful. I mean if you are hungry, you worked your ass

off after a day, and you have a meal, a meal is not satisfactory. You get angry, you get full, but you are not satisfied, pay you some more? Recognise what pleases you. Whatever meal it is, cheap or expensive, it must have the "mission accomplished" feeling. You know you have a connection with food. It is not just about filling you up. It is about a culture that you are partaking, a part of your culture.

Arnold: And that explains why you firmly believe there is only good food and bad food? Nothing in between?

Seetoh: All else is nonsense. PR nonsense.

Arnold: Is the PAP pro-food?

Seetoh: (long pause) Well, they have a minister in charge of the hawker centres so there must be some food lover up there. I do know of some ministers who would not mind dying with a plate of char kway teow in their hands. Of course our Prime Minister cannot eat randomly; he has to watch his health. But, did you know our founding father, Lee Kuan Yew's family is a food family? I think his grandfather came from Indonesia. Anybody know where they came from in Indonesia? No one knows this, right? You only know he stays at Oxley Rise, right? They came from Bangka, Google, Google Bangka, a little island full of Hakkas in Indonesia. How do I know? His brother told me. Very funny story. His brother is a very relaxed guy and looks totally like him, just about a foot shorter. He is a partner in this landscaping company which always invites us to curate the food for its events sometimes. So I was there and he was telling me, "Ah, my father… whenever I invite him for food events, he will show up." He said, "The best thing my grandfather did was to ask them to go to Singapore." If the grandfather did not say that, we would not have a Lee Kuan Yew today.

Anyway, the MM's family, you know, they invite top chefs from around the world to cook in his house, or in their restaurant. I know some of these obscure but very talented cooks around, cook for the Prime Minister, the then Prime Minister. Three or four, you string them together. That guy has makan parties you know. A Japanese chef will close the restaurant and invite Justin Quek to do this, the street food experts from Vietnam to do this. So they enjoy their food.

Arnold: What about hawker centres. Do they help preserve and promote Singapore's food culture?

Seetoh: Hawker centres are not about preserving culture. They openly

said it, it's to make sure that you and your children still have your $3 chicken rice in years to come. Unconsciously, they stumbled upon the fact that they have to preserve the culture. So they are also looking at the soft aspects of managing the hawker centre, not just licensing. They are looking at ways to give a special schooling, special deals to a new generation who want to come in and be street food professionals who can perhaps take on Gordon Ramsay again.

Audience: Many eateries here are franchises. It isn't really street food anymore. All we see opening now are new franchises but the same old, like, brands. Does this spell death for new eateries and cafes?

Seetoh: There are 2 types of people in the food business. One sells food, and the other does business. Crystal Jade and Paradise Group are doing business. Not only are their stalls franchised or what, even their sauces are franchised. I know of at least three big seafood chains that use the same chilli crab sauce from one supplier. You go to the big hawkers and seafood chains, notice that their chilli crabs are suspiciously similar? Even roti prata. Anybody who wants to start a stall, very easy, you call the supplier to

send one box of 300 pre-made roti prata balls, from a box. That guy will teach you how to flip. You just make your own curry, which is why so many roti prata stalls also taste suspiciously similar. Watch for the good ones that make their own dough. They have a big ball and pull from it, those are the ones that have a distinct difference. So your question about whether this is the cancer of our food culture? Yes, in one aspect it is. But my question is, what are you going to do about it?

Audience: Do you think queuing is part of the food culture in Singapore or should people put their time to better use?

Seetoh: When you are queuing up, you are waiting to be pleasured. What else do you want? You sit there and you reflect on life. When the plate of Lor Mee comes and you wallop the food, all is good. What do you want to do during that time? Update your Facebook or bitch about something? What you should fear is that while you are queuing up, the hawker will switch off the light and say "Bo Liao" (sold out). You should pray, pray that won't happen…. Pray and work. *Ora et Labora*. Bo Liao. Those two dreaded words.

Doctor

Tony Tan Keng Yam

President of the Republic of Singapore

Biography of The President

Dr Tony Tan Keng Yam was born in Singapore on 7 February 1940. He received his early education in St Patrick's School and St Joseph's Institution. Dr Tan graduated from the University of Singapore with a First Class Honours Degree in Physics in 1962, and went on to the Massachusetts Institute of Technology, where he obtained a Master of Science degree. He later obtained a PhD in Applied Mathematics at the University of Adelaide.

Dr Tan started his career as a lecturer with the Physics Department of the University of Singapore in 1964, after obtaining his Master of Science degree. He joined the University again as a lecturer with the Department of Mathematics after obtaining his doctorate in 1967. In 1969, he left the University to begin a career in banking with the Overseas-Chinese Banking Corporation (OCBC), where he rose to become General Manager. He left OCBC in 1979 to enter politics.

Dr Tan was elected as a Member of Parliament in 1979 and was appointed Senior Minister of State in the Ministry of Education. From October 1983 to January 1985, Dr Tan served as the Minister for Finance and concurrently as the Minister for Trade and Industry. From January 1985 to December 1991, he served as the Minister for Education.

In December 1991, Dr Tan stepped down from the Cabinet to return to the private sector as Chairman and Chief Executive Officer of OCBC. Dr Tan rejoined the Cabinet in August 1995 and was appointed Deputy Prime Minister and Minister for Defence. In August 2003, Dr Tan was appointed Deputy Prime Minister and Co-ordinating Minister for Security and Defence.

Dr Tan championed the development of higher education in Singapore as Minister for Education, Minister-in-charge for National University of Singapore and Nanyang Technological Institute (1981–1983) and Deputy Prime Minister overseeing higher education (1995–2005). Under Dr Tan's guidance, university education in Singapore became more globalised and was made accessible to more Singaporeans regardless of their family or financial background.

Dr Tan was also part of the trade union movement. He was appointed Chairman of NTUC Investment and Cooperative Committee in 1979 and served as Chairman of the Board of Trustees of NTUC Income from 1980 to 1991.

In 1988 Dr Tan was awarded the NTUC Medal of Honour by the National Trade Union Congress.

Dr Tan retired from the Cabinet in September 2005 and was appointed Deputy Chairman and Executive Director of the Government of Singapore Investment Corporation Private Limited (GIC), Chairman of the National Research Foundation and Deputy Chairman of the Research, Innovation and Enterprise Council, and Chairman of Singapore Press Holdings Limited (SPH).

In July 2011, Dr Tan stepped down from his positions at the GIC and SPH to contest in the Presidential Election. He was elected on 27 August 2011, and sworn in as the seventh President of the Republic of Singapore on 1 September 2011.

Dr Tan has been conferred numerous honours for his work. He was awarded the Foreign Policy Association Medal by the New York Foreign Policy Association for his outstanding leadership and service in both the public and private sectors. For his contributions towards Singapore's development into a global hub of scientific research and education in his earlier roles as Education Minister and subsequently as Chairman of the National Research Foundation, Dr Tan was inducted into the Honorary

Senate of the Foundation Lindau Nobelprizewinners Meetings in July 2012. Dr Tan was also awarded the Great Gold Medal by Comenius University (Slovakia) and the King Charles II Medal by the Royal Society of United Kingdom. He has honorary doctorates from the Loughborough University, Murdoch University, University of Sheffield and University of Adelaide.

Dr Tan married Madam Mary Chee Bee Kiang in 1964. They have four children (three sons and one daughter) and five grandchildren.

Speech by President Tony Tan Keng Yam at the Closing of the 2nd Fullerton–SJI Lecture Series on 5 November 2013

I would first like to thank the Organising Committee for inviting me to close the second series of the Fullerton-SJI lectures.

In this second series of lectures, the Organising Committee has put together a slate of distinguished speakers — Professor Leo Tan, Mr Richard Magnus, Mr Tony Chew, Mr Jeremy Monteiro, Br. Armin A. Luistro and Mr KF Seetoh — all of them established leaders in their own fields. We have benefitted from their candour and generosity in the sharing of their thoughts and experiences. Their experiences are different but they all share a common theme: whether one's chosen field is in the academic, public, business or creative sectors, a wholehearted pursuit of one's passion is vital not only for personal success but also for leadership.

Lasallian Education

As an old boy, I benefitted from the Lasallian education, first in St Patrick's School and then in SJI. It has been many years but I remain grateful till this day to my teachers and the La Salle Brothers who taught us to be the best that we can be, to lead useful lives and to contribute to society. By example, they showed us what it really meant to be people of integrity and people for others. At St Patrick's and SJI, in addition to learning life skills and academic knowledge, we experienced the meaning of service to the community, the importance of respecting differences of views, and the value of diversity.

SJI was founded more than 160 years ago on the vision of the Reverend Father Jean-Marie Beurel to serve everyone in our multi-racial, multi-religious society. I am glad that SJI to this day still adheres to Father Beurel's vision although SJI has gone through many changes to adapt to an evolving educational landscape and to meet the needs of newer generations of students. In the Lasallian tradition, SJI continues to embrace all members of our community regardless of race, language, creed or religion. SJI students are taught to see themselves as part of a larger community, and to serve all segments of our society. These Lasallian values are timeless and remain as relevant today as in Father Beurel's time.

Singapore's Development as a Nation

Similarly, Singapore has also seen many changes over the past 48 years. After gaining independence in 1965, we faced many challenges as a nation. We did not have natural resources or a hinterland to provide for a young and growing population. Unemployment was high and our people did not have adequate access to housing and education.

Nevertheless, through hard work, good policies, persistence and resilience, we did not give up — we went from third world to first world in one generation. Today, we have virtually full employment, nine out of ten Singaporeans live in their own homes, and young Singaporeans have a wide range of education opportunities up to the tertiary level. We have good infrastructure, especially our sea and air ports which are world class, and our public services are efficient.

As we develop, new challenges will continue to emerge. We cannot stand still. Our population is aging, and as our economy matures, we must expect our economy to slow down. Thus far, we have benefitted from globalisation as a small and open economy, and today's flatter and more interconnected world brings both opportunity and vulnerability. We have to surmount these challenges.

I am confident that Singapore will continue to do well despite these issues because we are today, in a stronger position to face these challenges in the future and we have good economic fundamentals. Our workforce is better educated and better-trained than before, and we have invested in Research & Development to stay competitive into the future.

Protecting Our Financial Reserves

As our economy grows through financial prudence and discipline, we have built up ample Financial Reserves to ensure a stable currency and to buffer Singapore in times of crisis. We have seen how crucial our financial reserves were for a small nation like Singapore, without natural resources that is heavily dependent on international trade and finance during the last Global Financial Crisis from 2008 till 2010. Then, to shore up confidence in Singapore's financial institutions amid a deepening credit crisis which was world-wide, Singapore was able to provide a guarantee on all bank deposits from October 2008 till 2010, which was backed by $150 billion from our Financial Reserves. When the global economic environment deteriorated further in January 2009, $4.9 billion from the reserves was drawn for the first time in our history to tide Singapore through the crisis by funding extraordinary measures, to encourage employers to keep workers on their payrolls and to boost bank lending to cash-strapped companies. So unemployment did not rise very high and we were one of the first to recover from the crisis because of these measures which were possible only because we have strong Financial Reserves. By 2011, the Government had put back into the reserves the amounts drawn down to fund the extraordinary measures taken during the economic crisis.

On an annual basis, our Financial Reserves also generate income that supplements our budgets to meet our increasing social expenditures without affecting our economic competitiveness. With effect from FY2009, under the Net Investment Returns (NIR) framework, up to 50% of the expected long-term real rate of returns on the relevant assets specified in the Constitution can be taken by the Government for spending. The NIR now contributes around 15–16% of the Government Expenditure.

As the President, I am responsible for ensuring the integrity of the Reserves and I will continue to make sure that the Financial Reserves are used judiciously for the benefit of Singaporeans now and into the future.

Building Up Our Social Reserves

Economic growth and financial stability remain fundamental to Singapore's progress and prosperity. But they are not everything. However, for Singapore to continue developing and to thrive as a nation, we need something more — something that I would like to call "Social Reserves".

To use a simple analogy, our Financial Reserves are like the piggy bank of a family and Social Reserves are the bonds that unite the family. The Social Reserves of a nation are the intangible ties that bind us to one another, and which make a nation greater than the sum of the individual citizens. Social reserves are the goodwill that makes us look out for one another even during difficult times, they are the resilience to overcome challenges and constraints, and they give us tenacity to progress as individuals and as a nation.

Financial Reserves are tangible and can be tracked to ensure that it grows, Social Reserves are intangible and we will only know how much we have when we need to draw on it. Just this year, we saw a good example of how we drew on this Social Reserves — during the Haze period, I was very encouraged that Singaporeans looked out not only for themselves, but also for one another. Masks were available but teams of volunteers made it possible to distribute them quickly to those in need.

While it is the responsibility of the Government to operate with financial discipline and fiscal prudence, and we can engage professionals to manage and grow our Financial Reserves, every Singaporean must be involved in growing our Social Reserves. We cannot leave Social Reserves in the care of others. Individually, we decide how to tend and grow our Social Reserves.

For example, our cultural diversity and vibrancy is our strength and we all must play our part in maintaining the mutual respect for the different languages, traditions and religions in our midst. Singapore has welcomed people from all over the world as a trading port since the 14th century. Like SJI, which embraces students from any race or creed, inclusiveness is a cornerstone of our society. Singapore is and must remain as an open economy to continue to generate opportunities for all. As citizens in a multi-cultural and global city, every Singaporean has a part to play in enhancing the understanding of and respect for the different cultures among us.

Another way that Singaporeans can contribute towards our Social Reserves is to care for the people around us. As President, I have the privilege to meet people from many walks of life, many professions, different backgrounds and age groups. I have been encouraged by many Singaporeans who serve the communities around them, whether it is in their workplaces, schools or neighbourhoods. I am happy that SJI continues to emphasise community service to build up our boys to become "Men for Others". Last year, I expanded the President's Challenge beyond fundraising to also promote volunteerism and social entrepreneurship. I hope that the President's Challenge will contribute towards building stronger Social Reserves by encouraging our people to do what we can, no matter how big or small, and to look out for one another, especially the needy — as SJI says, the last, the least and the lost.

Conclusion

Our Financial Reserves, comprising fiscal surpluses accumulated over the years, are akin to our savings in the bank, which we draw on in emergency situations and for funding of future needs. Our Social Reserves define who we are as a nation and we draw upon them for resilience and stability in any crisis, not just financial crisis.

There is a connection between Financial Reserves and Social Reserves. Financial Reserves supports our economic growth which generates the resources for our investments in various social institutions such as the HDB estates, our schools and universities, and national service, which help build up our Social Reserves. In turn, our Social Reserves support our hopes and dreams for future generations, create a conducive environment for economic growth and ensure that no one is left behind as Singapore progresses.

Both Financial Reserves and Social Reserves reinforce each other, to continue creating opportunities for Singaporeans, particularly the young.

Every Singaporean has the opportunity to help the country build up our Social Reserves by building trust and caring for one another in good times and in bad. We support one another so that we can become the best that we can be and build a future for ourselves and future generations.

Thank you once again for inviting me today to close the speaker series. I look forward to interacting with all of you later at the reception.

Forum

Arnold Gay: Mr President, once again, thank you very much for being our Guest of Honour today. There are a few interesting subsets in your speech which I hope to be able to press you on. But allow me first to frame today's lecture, it's going to be a little bit different. In the first series, and in the first six lectures of the second series, at this stage we invite questions from the floor. But as you can see, because we had such an overwhelming response to this particular session, we actually invited all the principals to get students to ask the questions in advance, hopefully, we are hoping to group them all together, and in the process, answer as many questions as possible, as opposed to taking questions from the floor. That's how we are going to be doing it today, if you are okay with it, Mr President?

So we can begin now, Mr President? Let me ask you first of all, on the speech, there are a few interesting things there — I will press you on about Lasallian education, you touched on the economy, but you also touched on something which I supposed is relatively new and this is the concept of having social reserves. Can you elaborate, are we lacking in this? How can we build on this, as a nation, as Singaporeans, and as young Singaporeans in particular?

President Tony Tan: Thank you Arnold. A nation needs many things. Fundamentally, a nation needs a strong economy to generate the financial resources needed to look after its people. What I am trying to do in my speech is to point out that a nation does not exist only on its financial reserves or its strong economy. A nation is its people and the people must look out for one another like members of a family. Just as intangible bonds bind the members of the family, individual citizens in a nation must be connected by social bonds. It is inevitable that we will face challenges as we go along and you need that intangible ties for our people to fight for the nation. In that way, we will be stronger and this is especially critical when we are hit by crises like the haze and SARS.

It is how we respond during major crises that the world gets an idea of who we are as a people. For example, in the case of the recent Tsunami which struck Japan, many people were killed and homes were flooded, but the people responded calmly. There was no looting and the... people helped one another. Of course, Japan has developed this over centuries as a nation whereas Singapore is still a young nation. But this is what we must have because it is inevitable that we will face crises in the future.

We have a good foundation to build strong ties with one another. Fundamental to all of this of course is our multi-racial, multi-religious, multi-cultural harmony. It is very important and we must never lose it. We have made great efforts to ensure that everyone has his or her space to practice individual beliefs, while maintaining the common spaces which everybody shares. When you look around the world, you can see the strife which occurs in countries with different races and different religions. But there is peace within Singapore because of the very intentional efforts by the Government and the community involving various racial groups and organisations to ensure that we understand and respect one another as Singaporeans. And that is something, which is to me, very important. It is fundamental, and we should never allow ourselves to forget that.

There are other areas, where we may have to do our little bit as individuals. As Singapore has become more affluent today, people feel less keenly the need to work together compared to the earlier years of Singapore's independence when survival was at stake. This is reflected in the "not in my backyard" syndrome which has surfaced recently regarding the building of nursing homes and old folks' homes. People know that these are needed but do not want them near their homes.

We have to think about such matters collectively, and balance individual needs with the needs of the community.

All of this is intangible and impossible to track. But it is very real and will help Singapore grow not just in the economic sense, but also in the social and national aspects. So social reserves is a nice way to summarise all of these intangible ties, and that is what I've tried to do during the speech — to have this concept to balance the financial reserves, which is much easier to explain.

Going ahead of course, there are many areas which we have to work on. We have to encourage an innovative and an enterprising spirit in Singapore. The US

for example is a very self-reliant people. They may have setbacks but they always bounce back because there is a strong sense of self-help and initiative among the people there. These are national characteristics which evolve over a period of time and we all have to work on it together. The point which I made in my speech is that we cannot leave this to somebody else. This involves all of us, and every citizen, every individual has a responsibility to try his or her best to help us build a stronger nation in Singapore.

Arnold: Thank you Mr President. We have a couple of questions here, in fact, three questions here that focus on Lasallian education.

1. The first one is from a student of SJI International: "Mr President, having gone through a Lasallian education yourself, to what extent would you emphasise the importance of the core Lasallian values towards raising a successful, well-rounded generation?"

2. Another question related to Lasallian values and education as well, this is another SJI International student: "As you used to be a true Lasallian, do you think we can apply Lasallian values, not only in our school life, but also in our career in the future?"

3. And one more question from an SJI International student: "Lasallian spirit is very apparent in most of Lasallian schools. We have a very important vision and mission to help the last, the lost, the least. In your opinion, how would you promote the Lasallian values to other communities so that together we can all help each other?

President: Rather than answering each question individually because they are all interconnected, I'll answer all of them once and talk about the Lasallian education. I believe that the values which the La Salle Brothers taught are timeless. They embody the spirit of service and the Brothers live up to these values through the lives which they lead. I remember vividly, in my education in St Patrick's and St Joseph's how they embodied the values of service to others. Of course, they did not neglect the educational skills and the need to strive for excellence but they went beyond that. They tried to give to the students a sense that each student is not only a person in himself but a member of the community. The Brothers went out of their way to interact with the students and to pass on these values.

I'm happy that in St Patrick's and SJI today these values are still there. The values will continue to stand you in good stead even when you leave school. The brothers promoted what I will call today "Holistic Education". One thing, for example, they were very keen on sports. Every afternoon when I was in school, the Brothers will join us in sporting activities. And they believed in this Latin saying "Mens sana in corpore sano" — healthy mind in a healthy body. They also taught the need to have good relationships with people, strive for excellence, strive to help others, becoming men of integrity and men for others.

The point is that they did not just spout these values; they actually live them through their interactions. How does it help you when you leave school? It gives you a compass, it gives a direction in your life, and it gives you what you call a purpose-driven life so that you know that whatever you do has an impact not only on yourselves but also on your families and other people. No matter where you are, no matter how you are placed, you can always find a niche in order to help others and this will be a constant standard by which you can live out.

The Lasallian tradition of education is something which is very much embedded. It goes back to the founder Fr Beurel, who was actually not a De La Salle Brother. He was a French priest but he asked the De La Salle Brothers to run the school because he knew that they were the best people to operate the system. They went back and forth between Singapore and France to raise money. Fr Beurel used his own money to buy a house so that the girls could be educated in the convent. This is not something which you learn from speeches or being told. You actually learn it from how the Brothers lived and you learn it from the teachers.

I hope that this spirit will continue in the Lasallian schools which I believe they are. It is important to have all of these values in addition of course to working hard, which we all have to do, and being the best that we can be. You will never regret living by the Lasallian values,

which will be a guide and a compass in your life. I think as you grow older, as I am growing older, they become even more relevant.

Arnold: Mr President, you touched on the financial crisis, and you touched on the resilience of the Singapore economy in your speech, and we do have quite a lot of questions that focus on the global economy and the Singapore economy. This is a bunch of questions that was put together by Mr Stephen Ng, I think he is a teacher at CHIJ St Theresa's Convent, to paraphrase all the questions, they are as follows:

1. Many have predicted that the next economic crisis would be any time soon, and even though we were able to safely survive the last one, what are your views on how Singapore would take on the challenge of the next economic crisis, if it were to happen?

2. The second one is a little more specific, the student wants to know, "What impact will global rising interest rates have on Singapore's economy?"

3. And the last one comes from CHIJ Toa Payoh: "Will the US economy still have the same kind of impact on the Singapore economy in 5 years' time?

Will Singapore be able to sustain economic growth in the next 50 years?

Maybe two parts there about interest rates, and the resilience in 5 years and in 50 years?

President: I don't know where to start. These questions are so broad and there is so much ground to cover, that I think it's difficult to do justice to the questions. Perhaps what I can do is to talk a little bit about the global economy and about the major economies and their prospects.

The world went through a financial crisis in 2008, 2009, and 2010. It was very difficult. I mentioned in my speech we had to come up with extraordinary measures to keep the Singapore economy going. Banks were failing and we ourselves went through a very difficult time. The process of healing from that financial crisis took a long time. There were many false starts because regulations have to be revised, banks have to be strengthened and capital has to be increased — these take time. It was a wrenching period for all countries. After five years of very difficult times, I think that we are now approaching the period when we have emerged from the financial crisis, and are moving into more normal times. Not that all the problems

have been resolved but at least we are not in as desperate a position as we were in 2008 and 2009.

Among the major economies around the world, the US was very hard hit because of a collapse in property prices and a credit crunch. Several banks were on the verge of failing, consumer confidence fell and the economy went flat. All of these events meant that it took time for confidence to recover. Today we are seeing a greater sense of confidence in the US economy. Credit demand has increased, the property market there has stabilised, and companies are expanding, though not as much as the Fed or the US government would like to see. Unemployment is still present but it is stabilising. Economic growth has resumed after a difficult period and maybe in the next few years it could reach 2.5 to 3%, which is quite good. Though not as high as before, it is at least better than in 2008 and in 2009. The vitality of the US business sector is still there. The US economy continues to generate new enterprises. It always amazes me how resilient the US economy is, despite all the problems that they have. I think they are on the road to recovery.

The situation in Europe a few years ago was so difficult that the people thought that the Eurozone could not survive. It may break up, and countries may exit the Eurozone. Some countries in the Eurozone were in desperate financial straits, and by and large, the Eurozone as a whole went into a deep recession. It took some years for the governments there to stabilise the economies but very severely austere budgets were imposed which caused a lot of unemployment. Since then, I think the recession is bottoming out. We are seeing glimpses of growth in Europe. The problems are still there but the determination of the European countries, particularly the major countries, to keep the Eurozone together is unmistakable. I think that this is more reassuring.

Asia had its difficulties, but we still are fortunate enough to be in a region which is fundamentally growing and has a lot of opportunities. Singapore has taken advantage of that growth though it has been a little bit dampened because it is inevitable that demand for goods produced by the region will decline as the developed economies buy fewer goods. The economies of Asian countries will slow down but certainly not to the same extent as in Europe or in the US.

So by and large, the world looks better today than 4 or 5 years ago but it does not mean that all the problems have been resolved and it is all clear skies ahead. There are still some risks, which could derail this continuing growth. For

example, in the US, as you know, there was a government shutdown because Congress was unable to pass for some weeks the raising of a debt ceiling, which caused a great deal of anxiety. They have done that now, but this is only until early next year and it will always be a worry to have this type of management when you are not sure how the US budget will be passed and what measures would still be in place. And of course, the raising of the debt ceiling is crucial to maintaining the credibility of the US dollar. Nobody can tell what will happen and we will have to wait and see but I remain optimistic that things will be resolved well. They have to be, otherwise, all of us will be in big trouble.

In order to get the economies going, the central banks have all resorted during the 2008 and 2009 period to what they call "monetary easing", that is to provide ample funds to the market to bring interest rates down to unprecedented levels. They bought bonds from the banks and so flooded the economy with liquidity. Of course this has a stimulative effect on the economies but this cannot go on forever. At some stage, this "monetary easing" has to stop and people now are talking about the "tapering off effect". It is always a worry for people whether this will be done without a glitch — otherwise there will be hiccups in the world economy. It is something which I know

is occupying the minds of governments and central banks, like the Fed and the ECB. It is something which has to be managed quite carefully, but all in all, they have done well so far. We hope they will be able to manage this successfully, and bring about the normalisation of interest rates as well as normal monetary policies.

The Eurozone is stronger now and there is less worry of a breakup. But some countries, like Greece, still need assistance and you have to see whether the sentiment in Europe is towards a strong Eurozone where the countries that are doing better will help the countries in need, and of course with measures to ensure that it is not just money down the drain. So far, countries like Germany and France have shown that they are determined to keep the Eurozone together and we don't hear about the exits from the Eurozone now. But it still remains precarious and you do not know whether some crisis will arise out of political, or fiscal or taxation or monetary issues, so I think that is something to watch out for.

From time to time, there are worries like the flight of capital from the emerging markets. Nowadays, as more currencies are floated, such capital flows are more manageable, and I don't think we will get a repetition of the crises we saw in the

1960s or 1970s. Countries have taken steps to undertake reform. Even Japan has made a remarkable turnaround under Prime Minister Abe to simulate the economy, relax some of their regulations and encourage participation of women in the labour force. I think this is hopeful. China has gone through a successful leadership transition and continues to power Asian growth. So, there is a relatively better scope for growth than before — not entirely plain sailing and there are possibly some problems ahead — but overall the economy is in a better shape than 4 or 5 years ago.

Arnold: Thank you Mr President. The next series of questions actually relate to what you had just spoken about in terms of where the global economy is, and that is the role of innovation, research and development. You have long been a long proponent of all these.

1. A question from an SJI International student here is that, in a country largely dependent upon its human capital Singapore, is entrepreneurial spirit and innovation the way forward? How is this being fostered at a national level?

2. Another question from an SJI International student: If we can train and train our innovative spirit, can you suggest us something we could start working on? As a young Singaporean I presume?

3. And we also have a very long one from CHIJ Toa Payoh: "How can innovation in Singapore help the economy down the road?" Like natural resources as we touched on earlier. "Apart from students, who else plays an important role in inculcating the innovative spirit in Singaporeans and making sure that it continues in Singapore in the foreseeable future?"

President: I think it would be helpful if I were to approach this topic of innovation within the context of how the Singapore economy has developed. In the 1960s and 1970s, when we had high levels of unemployment and people did not have high-level skills, we had a labour-intensive economy basically to just provide jobs for people. As our economy developed and labour became tighter, Singapore moved into what we call a capital-intensive industry, which used more capital, and productivity increased with fewer workers. But you can't keep on investing in order to promote growth, as China is now finding out. So we are now into the third phase — what you call the knowledge economy, which not only builds products, but generates and translates ideas into saleable goods and services. And to do that, we need to have people, not only scientists or researchers, but everyone in Singapore, particularly our young people, to have an innovative spirit and improve whatever fields we are working in.

On the government side, what the government has done for many years now is to invest massively in research and development. In the recent years, we have world-class researchers in an array of fields, including new technologies like 3-dimensional printing, as well as genomics. Now there are new areas which are very promising, like Big Data, which uses massive data collected from various sources in order to predict trends, which has led to a whole new area of business analytics to sort of make sense out of the mass of data.

But I don't think that you can say that we depend only on R&D and researchers to create a knowledge economy. I think in whichever field that you are in, you can always try to see how you can improve things. I always say that young people are better at this game, and they have an added advantage because they do not know that what they want to do is impossible and that's wonderful, because they are willing to try! Yes, they may fail from time to time, but this is a learning experience and they must have this spirit of wanting to try new things. It doesn't mean that they need to do a grand project. I have met many young people who have started small social enterprises, such as businesses to develop products for autistic kids. I think these are good ideas and we should encourage this spirit of trying and of improving. It's not a matter of waiting until you have the skill; it also requires a mindset change. I think we should inculcate that in Singapore.

I am very hopeful for our young people. When I talk to them, I always encourage them to look forward and to try, and I would encourage all of you to do the same. Whatever field you are in, whatever subject you are doing, whatever place you are in, there's always room for improvement. The government I'm sure will do its best in order to provide necessary resources, but fundamentally it is something in which people need to help themselves and see how they can help others. And I think R&D and innovation is something which has to be in our DNA if Singapore is to continue to progress and thrive in the coming years.

Afterword

✧ Vincent Anandraj

The celebration of the individual within a community of learners has always been the hallmark of Lasallian education. The success of this focus on developing leaders is clearly borne out in the number of SJI Old Boys who have held, are holding and will continue to hold, senior positions in Politics, Public Service, Education, Business, Sports, Arts and Entertainment and Law amongst a whole host of other fields.

At the core of any discussion on Leadership, I believe, should be the topic of "Human Capital" — a phrase that seems to be synonymous with, and closely associated to, leadership.

Human beings have always looked to individuals to lead the way; the destination being secondary, as the steps that are taken, define that destination. It is important though to note that leadership does not only happen in situations of crisis but that opportunities to exercise leadership occur on a daily basis.

Being a fan of football and in particular, a fan of the Fantasy Football League, where one creates one's dream team, I pondered this question: What sort of company/institution would it be if you had all of the six Leaders, who have spoken in this Second Series, working in it?

In this fantasy team, let's call it Lasalle United, we would have:

Playing upfront in a striker's role, Prof Leo Tan — known for his constant search of an opportunity.

Playing in the full-back position, Richard Magnus — known for his stability and reliability.

Orchestrating the team we would have team-captain and midfield maestro Tony Chew — known for his readiness to rally the troops and get stuck in.

Dazzling with his silky skills on the wing would be Jeremy Monteiro — with his innate ability to create chances out of thin air.

With the experience of educating 21 million students in 46,000 schools, the team manager would be Bro Armin Luistro — known for his focus on detail.

Finally, in goal, we would have KF Seetoh, known for his flair and his "throw caution to the wind" attitude.

The common denominator — anyone from this team would be able to step in for their team-mates as they are multi-faceted. They would not stand still, they would not take no for an answer, they would not shy away from leading, they would not be backward in coming forward, they would drive and keep the momentum. They are all "men with others and men for others."

Their experiences at SJI, which have seeped into their DNA, have made these leaders individuals who would take others along and never become disconnected. They fasten themselves to their missions and while sailing close to the wind, chart new courses. Marcus Buckingham, in his book *The One Thing You Need to Know: ... About Great Managing, Great Leading, and Sustained Individual Success*, is emphatic about this, *"Above all else, they must never forget the truth that of all the human universals — our need for security, for community, for clarity, for authority, and for respect — our need for clarity... is the most likely to engender in us confidence, persistence, resilience, and creativity."*

Prof Leo Tan recalled the time he showcased how seizing opportunities to be a leader affords you a platform from which to effect change and also to be that change. He said at his lecture, *"The essence in leadership* is not about leading people. It's about getting out there and doing what you can, what you think cannot be done. But nothing is impossible until it is proven to be impossible."

Warren Bennis in his much-cited work, *On Becoming a Leader*, states "*People begin to lead that moment when they decide for themselves how to be.*" Prof Leo developed Bennis' statement by adding, "*So I remember that discipline, honest hard work and using creativity — which the Lasallian spirit embodies — is embedded in the culture of La Salle. Using the creativity which is ingrained in us, to the fullest of our ability would ensure that first, we will have a bright future, second, our society will have a bright future, and third, our country and the world will be a better place to be in.*" The impact of an individual on a nation.

Richard Magnus, in a very stimulating lecture, shared his views on "*the new leadership*", "*We often hear people say that we need a new leadership style for this century. In a globalising world with a better educated workforce and constituency that is no longer inclined to be seen and not heart, a new leadership is in fact called for, but style is not the key leadership issue. Substance is. It is about core behaviour on the job, not surface detail and tactics, a core that changes little over time, across different cultures,*

or in different industries or societies. Ethics, to me, is an essential core."

Richard summed up his lecture with the crucial line, "*You do what is right, right what is wrong, you bring hope when there is despair, you bring peace where there is none.*" The importance of a moral compass to keep us on the right course. Doug Lennick and Fred Kiel, in their work, *Moral Intelligence*, refer to how "*moral competence can indeed be enhanced throughout life. Competence shows up in behaviors. And when it comes to moral behaviors in the workplace, organizations can and must create environments within which the following principles of moral intelligence come to life: integrity, responsibility, compassion and forgiveness.*"

Tony Chew, a truly self-made man, reiterated the importance of having mentors. He underscored this in his lecture, "*First of all, I had a plan, a target, a vision, or perhaps just a dream. Secondly, I didn't do it alone. I had mentors, partners and colleagues, some of whom are here today. Thirdly I had a strong sense of commitment.*"

He elaborated on this, "*Once I made this decision (here he referred to his commitment to Singapore), it set my direction; it gave me a strong compass by which I made all my subsequent decisions.*" Dogged determination and a can-do attitude are critical facets of a leader.

Mentors are an important aspect of leadership, as John Buchan reminds us, "*The task of leadership is not to put greatness in humanity, but to elicit it, for the greatness is already there.*"

Jeremy Monteiro, the king of Jazz, also believed in the importance of seizing opportunities and having a passion, in leadership.

He mused, "*I think that being at SJI at the right time and the right place and the having the right talents are some of the many blessings I am very thankful for.*"

For budding musicians, Jeremy had this piece of advice, "*For anyone who has just even the least bit of talent in the music or arts, all you have to do is keep working on your craft on a constant basis, every day.*"

Summing himself up as a musician, "*I play the music I love, with the people I love, for the people who love me.*" Passion is essential for success and when you do something you are passionate about, it is a blessing.

Bro Armin Luistro, our International Lasallian speaker, spoke about the importance of being willing to follow if one wishes to lead. This approach is close to Max de Pree's assertion in *Leadership is an Art*, "*The first responsibility of a leader is to define reality. The last is to say thank you. In between the two, the leader must become a servant and a debtor. That sums up the progress of an artful leader.*"

The Secretary for Education for the Philippines shared, "*The moments in my life when I saw myself taking on leadership positions was because the one in front had either given up or absconded and ran way from the fight. I'm not the kind of person who would leave if the project is not finished. I believe leaders choose to put themselves in a box that reads: "First in, last out". I'm happy to wash the dishes after everyone has left the party. Sincerely, I'm that type of leader. And in these different situations in my life, including the advocacy for truth, it was only because there was no one else, and someone said "You'll be the spokesperson" and I said "I'll do it only until the next willing leader comes in."* The humility that inspires those who wish to be led.

Bro Armin's belief in leading by following has resonance with Bill George's statement in his book, *Why Leaders Lose Their Way*, "*Leaders can avoid these pitfalls by devoting themselves to personal development that cultivates their inner compass, or True North. This requires reframing their leadership from being heroes to being servants* of the people they lead. *This process requires thought and introspection because many people get into leadership roles in response to their ego needs. It enables them to transition from seeking external gratification to finding internal satisfaction by making meaningful contributions through their leadership."*

Mr Makan Guru himself, KF Seetoh amused the audience with his wide-ranging and deeply humorous speech but turned serious when he broached the topic of a leader being someone who keeps his feet and ears close to the ground.

When Seetoh was asked by the moderator, Arnold Gay, to talk about one quality that he felt was important in a leader, Seetoh had this to say, "*I am an observer. You can't talk about life and business if you don't observe. You can't just sit down with your laptop go onto Google and write reports. You walk the streets and look at people and take a look at their faces. Stand there and observe them with a kopi o at Lorong 18. You see how life is at that level, and people are at that level. You can hear their heartbeat and you get a lot of ideas. You grow up with that heartbeat there. That's where you get a lot of ideas."*

President Tony Tan, in his Closing Remarks, spoke about the impact his time at SJI had on his life and how it made him strive to make a difference to society. He drew a parallel between leaders who emerge from testing periods to Singapore's emergence from the many challenges of the early days of independence to its enviable First World status.

Touching on the way a leader draws people together, President Tony Tan elaborated on the need to shore up our "Social Reserves" which will see us through when challenges materialise. These reserves will ensure that Singapore remains a leader in building a future that we can all be proud of. He said, "*Every Singaporean has the opportunity to help the country build up our Social Reserves by building trust and caring for one another in good times and in bad. We support one another so that we can become the best that we can be and build a future for ourselves and future generations."*

Let me conclude by sharing the distilled version of what the leaders had shared, in no particular order:

1. True leaders do not lead in isolation.

2. Transformational leaders empower all their people by enabling their organisations to harness opportunities

when the seas are choppy and power personal growth and development in their staff when the water is calm.

3. Finally, modern day leaders are judged on their adaptability more than their ability to perform in a traditional role.

It has been an honour to Chair the Organising Committee for the Series and I would like to take this opportunity at this point to thank some individuals without whom, this remarkable Series would not have been possible:

Firstly, Michael Sng and Tan Tee How for their vision, Philip Ng of Far East Organisation for his unstinting support, Arnold Gay for being the consummate professional at being both the moderator and the co-editor of the book on the Series, The Fullerton Hotel Singapore for their wonderful hospitality and the Straits Times for being our Media Partner. A special thank you to Eliza Lim and Linda Yong for the administrative support and most importantly the students and Old Boys who have supported this.

It has been a singular privilege to learn from the leaders who have spoken during this Series and it is our wish that you are able to too. I will leave you with a quote by John Quincy Adams:

"*If your actions inspire others to dream more, learn more, do more and become more, you are a leader.*"

Vincent Anandraj
Class of 1986

www.ingramcontent.com/pod-product-compliance
Lightning Source LLC
Chambersburg PA
CBHW070344100426
42812CB00005B/1426